STUDY SENSE

WHAT MEMORY RESEARCH TELLS US ABOUT STUDYING IN COLLEGE

by

KRISTINA T. KLASSEN, M.S.

STUDY SENSE PUBLICATIONS

Cover Design and Illustrations by the author.

Printed by Omni Graphics, 7905 Meadowlark Way
Coeur d' Alene, ID 83815

ISBN 0-9700194-0-8

Copyright 2000 by Kristina T. Klassen
Published by Study Sense Publications

For information contact Study Sense Publications,
P.O. Box 652, Hayden, ID, 83835.

Please visit our World Wide Web site at *www.studysense.com*

For our children

James, Michelle, Jared, Rachel & Paul,

my original guinea pigs in the learning lab of life.

And for all students everywhere.

You can.

TABLE OF CONTENTS

INTRODUCTION
TURN ON YOUR MENTAL COMPUTER

In a corner of the SUB dining room, Margie sits with her friend Gina, staring at her textbook. In an hour she will take her chemistry test and she is panicked. Even though she has already spent 8 hours this week reading over her text and notes, she cannot seem to grasp the principles that are going to be on the test. Hovering between D and F, Margie is hoping against hope that somehow she can pull off a C by finals to avoid failing this class which is required for her major in veterinary science.

Sound familiar? This is a scene from college life repeated every semester, and it is no accident. Just like babies do not come born with instruction manuals, neither does the brain. It is like someone gave us a brand new computer setup with state of the art technology, modem, CD ROM, Internet access, and all of the latest bells and whistles...but no manual. What can we do?

Many students at the community college where I teach express the same frustrations to me every year. It is about time that we took a systematic, concrete look at how the mental process of study works to make the most of our college experience.

It all begins by asking the question, "What is study, anyway?" We use the term every day, but what does it mean?

To many of us the word *study* brings with it unsavory images, like inhumanely late nights, hours of reading, and the frustration of less than perfect grades after so much agonizing struggle. *Study* has gotten a negative reputation because it is an undefined activity with uncertain rewards. Even after putting in long hours there are no guarantees of good grades, so it can be discouraging and tempting to avoid. But it only seems to be hit and miss because we don't understand the fundamental process. Since study is based 100% on memory, there is no better way to learn this process than to see what memory researchers have discovered and apply their findings to our situation as students. That is what this little book is all about.

What do the experts say? Many noted memory researchers have spent years investigating how we remember. After countless hours of experimentation with different types of memory situations, they have concluded that it <u>doesn't matter</u> how much we **want** to learn, how much we **try** to learn, **how hard** the topic is, or **how much time** we spend on it. <u>If</u> we know **WHAT TO DO** with the course material, we will remember it. In other words, the single most important factor involved in memory is what we do with the material, not sincerity, difficulty, desire or time. Certainly, we must intend to learn, want to learn, spend time and rehearse, but these alone do not guarantee that we will remember. This is very encouraging. Since it is more a matter of WHAT to do with information, it is a skill that can be learned by anyone... regardless of intelligence or past experience.

Even though study is an individual enterprise and no two people are exactly alike, there are predictable rules that govern how our brains work and knowing those rules helps us make the best use of our time and effort. If you already have a study system that works for you, this book will explain why your technique is effective and will help you refine your methods. If you have not developed a workable system, this book will help you create a plan to succeed academically.

In either case, I hope that by the time you finish applying the principles we are going to discuss, that you will have accomplished five things:

1.　You will have an organized method / direction / plan for your task of study.

2.　You will have decreased your overall study time.

3.　You will be able to remember and apply entire concepts, rather than mere trivia.

4.　You will be earning consistent A's and B's in every one of your classes.

5.　You will actually enjoy the study process, because you feel like you have control and you are being successful.

I have called the book *Study Sense* because it only makes good sense to study in the way that your brain operates the best. Now, let's learn how to turn on and operate your mental computer.

SECTION I
THE BASICS

There are two principles that lay the groundwork for success and no amount of time spent learning individual techniques can compensate if these elements are not present. They are an active mental attitude and recognizing how this new task of college level study differs from our past academic experience. We need to be mentally geared for the job ahead and we need to understand just what it is we are doing.

PRINCIPLE #1: THE POWER OF ATTITUDE

The first basic factor is attitude about study. All disciplines recognize that an active mind-set is critical to success. To be involved passively is to fail.

For example, before any good sports team goes onto the field or court to play, what does a coach do? He sets an attitude. Games are won or lost in the locker room when an attitude is either set correctly to win or set for defeat. Study is no different.

ATTITUDE IS EVERYING

Rick, Harvey and Scott are roommates. They are in their first year at Ambition State University and went to high school together. All scored approximately the same on the SAT, about average for entering freshmen. All three guys are in the same classes, looking toward engineering degrees.

Every morning at 7, Rick wakes up and groans to himself, "Do I really have to go to class today?" He is particularly tired since he stayed up until 2 a.m. watching a movie. He spends the first 10 minutes of his day in bed, trying to think of ways he can get around attending his 8 o'clock class, Physics. Here are some of his regular morning thoughts:

1.   Prof. Mumble is so boring, I'll learn more if I just get the notes from Sam, because I'll only fall asleep in class.

2.   My mind will be more rested to study later if I stay in bed one more hour.

3.   Prof. M doesn't count attendance, so he'll never miss me.

4.   If I ace my higher level classes, this Introduction to Physics class won't count very much when I go to transfer to engineering school.

Needless to say, Rick only goes to class when he absolutely has to. When he is there he sits in the back of the room and doodles throughout the hour, only noting what the instructor says when he raises his voice or writes something on the board. Even then, he only writes down exactly what the teacher says. He does barely enough to meet the basic course requirements.

At exam time, Rick reads through his notes once, the first time he has read them since the lecture. "Why should I?" He reasons, "I have studied enough. Hey, I understand this stuff." At midterm, Rick is surprised to find a D+ for his Physics grade. Is he mad! "Boy, that Prof. M is really unfair! I did everything he required! I studied for that class and I really understood it! I want to drop Physics and take it from a different instructor next year. Maybe I'll get someone who knows how to teach!"

Sound familiar?

An attitude that asks, "Is this good enough?" does not work. Perhaps you have found this out.

Harvey has the same Physics class. He is trying "as hard as he can" to get an A. Every morning at 7 he is up and ready for school, but is sometimes late because he isn't very organized and can't always find his keys or his calculator. In class he sits wherever he can find a seat. He pays attention and takes notes. Harvey attends class regularly and reviews his notes and textbook before exams. He even reads late into the night to make sure that he is never behind in his course material. But at midterm, Harvey gets a B in Physics. He goes home dejected. As he enters the apartment he tells his roommates, "Boy, college sure is hard! I studied hours for this class and I can never get higher than an A-, and I only got that once. I have no more time I can spend. I guess I am not smart enough to get A's. Those guys who are on the Dean's list must be geniuses!"

An attitude that says, "I'm trying as hard as I can," doesn't get top grades, either. Maybe you have found that out, as well.

Scott is also in that Physics class. None of his relatives ever graduated from college. In fact, only one uncle ever graduated from high school. But Scott was determined to do whatever was necessary to get A's. He was going to succeed at college even if it killed him, so he made it a habit to discover and target all of his course requirements thoroughly and systematically. Everything he did was focused around organization for personal control of his efforts. Academic success was his top priority.

On Sunday night he would look at his assignment calendar and notice what topics he would be studying in all of his classes that week. Then he took 10 minutes or so and flipped through his textbooks, glancing over the pages of material that were assigned. After that, he packed his book bag for the next day and got a good night's rest, so his mind would be clear. In the morning he showered, shaved, ate and grabbed his bag. He was always relaxed and early for class. He consistently sat in the same seat in the front row because he said this kept him from being distracted.

During Prof. M's lecture he kept eye contact with him, listening through all of the monotone to try to understand how the professor was thinking and what steps he was explaining. His notes were a step by step recreation of Professor Mumble's picture of the material, including Scott's own summaries of the explanations. Then, after Physics, while he was waiting for his English class to begin, he read over Prof. M's notes and added things that would help him remember the ideas better when he read them later. He knew that if he didn't, he would forget them. It was always easier when he did this.

Later that same night, Scott reread his notes and then read the textbook pages on the same subject, making notes of his own as he read and jotting down questions as he found parts that he didn't understand. The next day, he went to Prof. M and asked him to explain the questions he had. As a result, he got to know how Prof. M thought and this made it even easier to understand him in class. He mapped out the course material so he could visualize it and was careful not to procrastinate on the assignments.

Scott asked Prof. M what type of tests he gave, so he could aim his study at the proper target. He also went over the course material regularly with another student in his class to make sure he understood it. He and his study partner each made up practice tests and swapped them,

> *discussing their answers. At midterm Scott got an A, but didn't tell his roommates because he didn't want them to think he was bragging.*

The only mental mind-set to have if you want to succeed is, "Whatever it takes."

So, if you are finding yourself saying, "Is this good enough?" or "I'm trying as hard as I can," that will partially explain why you're not getting top grades. To take control of the process and get consistent

PRIORITIES DETERMINE SUCCESS

A's, you MUST pull out all of the stops and assume the attitude, "Whatever it takes to succeed, I will do it." And DO it.

RULE OF THUMB
"IS THIS GOOD ENOUGH?" = C'S OR D'S
"I'M TRYING AS HARD AS I CAN." = B'S OR C'S
"WHATEVER IT TAKES." = CONSISTENT A'S

PRINCIPLE #2: THE 4 MAJOR CHALLENGES OF COLLEGE-LEVEL ACADEMICS

We also need to understand the 4 big differences between high school and college academics, which prove to be a freshman student's greatest challenges.

1. ***Active vs. passive mental approach.*** In the example above, Scott was taking an active mental approach to his classes. He realized his challenges and his limitations and actively set himself to work around them in an organized way. This ALWAYS works. Assuming that you can just plug in your old habits from years past and automatically succeed brings

much frustration and disastrous results.

In high school we were fairly inexperienced at higher level academics, and therefore somewhat passive thinkers as we learned the process. We were subject to teachers who fed us and expected us to regurgitate data back to them. We got A's for memorizing details and writing reports based on the ideas of others. Now, we are expected to be on an active search for understanding, mastering entire concepts and synthesizing massive amounts of information. First-year college students often find themselves hitting a *brick wall* when their old ways of studying no longer work.

     2.   ***Conceptual vs. incremental thinking.*** Thinking in concepts, rather than details is a definite skill one needs to acquire. Students who tend to be more spatial in interpreting the world find this less difficult, but the majority of students, the detail people, find this shift in mental focus a daunting challenge.

It feels like you will miss something if you interpret the course as an overview. But, guess what. If you understand the broad picture of what the instructor is communicating, details will fall into place and be far easier to remember. Exit rote memorization, which never amounts to much, anyway, and is usually not worth the time and effort.

     3.   ***Independent vs. dependent thought.*** We all like to think for ourselves. We looked forward to the day when we could express ourselves and get recognition for our brilliant ideas. Now, we are required to do just that. In most college courses, students are graded on their original synthesis of material, on personal understanding and higher level thinking. There are opportunities to do original research papers, prepare presentations, and write essay exams of a compare-contrast nature.

The student who remains in the mental mode of parroting back the text and notes is doomed to memorize tons of soon-forgotten details for little academic profit. Such students usually do not achieve higher than C+ status, because that is the grade for doing an average job well. Anyone can read a book and regurgitate it. It takes thought to handle college assignments successfully. That is what "higher education" is all about.

4.   *Comprehension vs. facts.* In high school, most classes are geared toward facts and details. Lack of experience and the cognitive limitations of adolescence limit the high school curriculum, especially in public schools, where there can be no elimination on the basis of ability. This often prevents teachers from requiring their students to comprehend material thoroughly. For example, I remember tutoring a B student in her high school history class. When I asked her how the teacher tested on the chapters, she showed me a list of 120 vocabulary terms that she had to memorize. No organization, no comprehension, just terms with no frame of reference.

When we reach the college level, details and definitions are used to support comprehension. If we haven't learned some way to integrate and synthesize facts and details while looking for meaning and understanding of the material, we will have a difficult time understanding what to do with course information.

SECTION II
STUDY IS...... [DEFINING THE TASK]

Now, we get to answer the question, "What is study?" It is something we need to do, but there is little solid help in explaining WHAT it is, much less HOW to do it. We may learn how to take notes, how to outline, and how to highlight the text, but is that all? Are we to sit in a silent library reading each line of a 500-page textbook until the information clicks into place automatically? Are we to write down every word the instructor says? Are we to memorize all of the information systematically? Or are we supposed to count study success by the number of pages our eyes have passed over, line by painful line?

None of the above.

We can eliminate the word *study* from our vocabulary <u>entirely</u> and replace it with the word *organization*. The person who wrote your textbook and your instructor both have in their minds an orderly organization of knowledge that they are trying to communicate to you

**STUDY IS
ORGANIZATION**

through words and pictures until you possess the same mental picture they have.

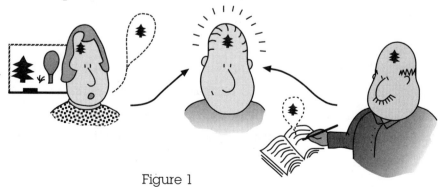

Figure 1

Once you have this picture, you can draw information from it for many different tasks and solve various problems. In fact, you can solve almost any problem that the instructor can throw at you because you are working from the same organized knowledge base. As you discover and clarify what you don't understand, you will fine-tune your mental organization. Then, all you need is repeated review (practice) to solidify the information mentally.

The main problem comes when we have not organized the material for ourselves. Why organization?

Organization is critical because researchers have isolated

ORGANIZATION = DISTINCTIVENESS

distinctiveness as the single factor necessary for 100% recall, and distinctiveness requires organization. That means that repetition without organization yields poor memory, while repetition with organization yields superior memory. So, organization MUST precede repetition or it's a waste of time.

If we don't organize first, we find ourselves having to *fine-tune* our understanding <u>as we go</u>, so that by the time we begin to get a fairly clear idea of what is going on, it is too late. We don't have a clear picture before we have to test

REPETITION WITHOUT ORGANIZATION = A WASTE OF TIME

out on it. That translates to C grades, at best.

Even if we do pass with a C, that still doesn't give us much of a knowledge base to tackle future problems or more advanced courses. So, the key to learning how to study is really learning how to better organize the subject, any subject. To do this we must understand our equipment, which is our memory.

The brain is like a computer, a high tech, electronic chip bank of unlimited capacity. Like a PC, you program it (encoding), hold the information (storage) and output when you need to use it (retrieval).

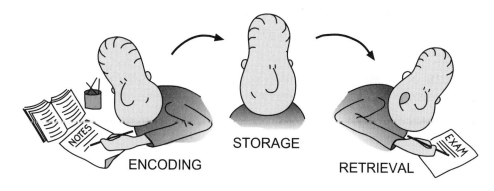

STORAGE

ENCODING

RETRIEVAL

Figure 2

With these three stages, it is how, **not** how much we program new material. It is your job as a programmer to encode all new information is such a way that it <u>can</u> be retrieved, in a <u>form </u>that allows you to use it whenever you need it. It would be a waste of time to encode information in a form that you couldn't access later.

There are also three levels of depth involved in memory storage. We store memories at either a superficial level, a level of understanding, or a level of practical use. The level we target in our study depends upon the type of test we will take, even though our end goal as students is to encode all information at the deepest level in order to remember more for the longest time. To enter each of these levels requires the techniques we will discuss in the following chapters.

Finally, memory depends upon nerve cells growing new connections between them when they are stimulated, and upon the permanent changes that occur when they are stimulated repeatedly the same way with time between sessions. I'll explain this as we go along.

What we call STUDY is simply the total effort of properly encoding new material to the required depth. We are constantly programming our computers in usable ways, and there are some rules to that programming, just as there are to any PC.

What follows is a practical explanation of these rules.

SECTION III
MAJOR MEMORY PRINCIPLES

CHAPTER 1 = IT'S ALL UNDER CONTROL

WHY CONTROL?

Our first task is to take active control. Why? Since stress reactions kill memory recall and stress always involves unpredictable and uncontrollable situations, we must do everything we can to establish total control over the study process. The body

> **STRESS REACTIONS KILL MEMORY**

chemistry involved in the stress reaction is a #1 memory killer. Our marvelous *fight or flight* stress response is built to save us from danger (like exams). When it is triggered, our muscles are primed to fight or run away, not to sit there and think. (Obviously, remembering facts and ideas is not the most necessary element in survival.) While adrenaline facilitates memory encoding, it is deadly to memory retrieval.

> **TEST ANXIETY IS A NATURAL, PHYSIOLOGICAL REACTION**

As a result, heavy amounts of adrenaline short-circuit our memory system and our mind is put on a physiological *hold.* This means that all of the gut-wrenching anxiety and brain freeze that we feel so intensely at exam time is absolutely normal. I have met many students who think that it only happens to them, or that something is wrong because they feel like this. Just knowing that it is a natural, physiological reaction helps a lot. (The <u>last</u> thing we need is to get anxious about being test-anxious.)

So to decrease our study anxiety, the first thing we must do is predict what will happen during the academic term ahead, to establish our control over it. (By the way, this is one big reason why procrastination is academic poison. You can find all four reasons in Appendix II at the end of the book.) We never feel so helpless, anxious and out of control as when we procrastinate.

Control also contributes to confidence. Researchers have long noticed a positive relationship between confidence and success. If you have control over a situation, you are more confident of your ability to handle it and the resulting controlled, organized activity becomes a self-fulfilling prophesy.

> **PREDICTION**
> **+**
> **CONTROL =**
> **FREEDOM FROM**
> **TEST ANXIETY**

The third thing control does is to allow distinctiveness to be developed. Since researchers have discovered that the single necessary and sufficient condition for 100% recall is distinctiveness (and to be distinct, information must be clear), we cannot say too much about mental clarity. This can only be achieved by mental control of study tasks.

How can we do this?

CREATING AN ORGANIZED ACTION PLAN

STEP #1 -- PREDICT COURSE TASKS

So, here you are at the beginning of the school year. Your tuition is paid, you have moved into your room, bought your books, and gone to your first set of classes. Now you are sitting down with the intention of "studying." What do you do first? [Remember, since study = organization, anything you can do to organize your academic efforts is part of the study process.]

First, take out all of the *syllabi* you have been given. These are the sets of rules governing every individual course that instructors pass out on the first day of class. As you have

> **IDENTIFY ALL THE WAYS TO MAKE POINTS**

gathered by now, after attending your first day of classes, not all courses operate according to the same rules. In each course, there are different ways to score points. Would you ever play an important game without knowing how to score?

Take a high-lighter and mark off what the exact course requirements are and how the grade is calculated. [For example, a course may be based primarily on exams, or exams may be minor and a final project may be 50% of your grade.] Course *elements* can be exams or quizzes, projects, class discussion & participation, attendance, workbooks, or any other course requirement. Pay attention to the percentages given to each particular element.

This will show you two things. First, it will tell you how to distribute your effort. For example, if exams are the major part, or all there are to the grade, you know that classroom

information and textbook content will be your primary focus.
Also, if a project or paper has a high percentage, you know to begin independent research early on in the term to produce a better product.

> **THE COURSE SYLLABUS IS A CONTRACT & A MAP**

Second, it helps you put your *grade package* together. Knowing how you are going to achieve the grade you need gives you CONTROL over your term.

Also, by paying attention to these details, you can avoid unnecessary disaster. For example, if you have a grade package that includes a sizeable percentage for attendance and you have a work commitment that may require you to miss class once a week, you will either need to ask your instructor if that requirement can be fulfilled in other ways, or change to a different section that has a smaller attendance component. Think ahead.

> **REMEMBER:**
> **IF YOU DON'T STUDY YOUR SYLLABI WITH YOUR GRADE GOAL IN MIND, IT'S LIKE PLAYING A GAME "JUST FOR FUN," NOT TO WIN.**

This is essential, because the syllabus is an agreement between the individual teacher and yourself to which both of you will be held accountable. You don't want to overlook this deed to your success in the course. Look at it as both a contract and a map. It will be your guide and comfort in the middle of the course, when you have forgotten what is due when, you don't know how to get the grade you need, you feel bogged down in mud, and you can't see the end for yourself.

STEP #2 -- PACE YOUR EFFORTS

Next, get yourself a large wall calendar, preferably one of those that can double as a desk pad. This will become your *master brain*. On this master, mark down <u>all</u> of your class times, work times, and other commitments for the term. Next, copy <u>all</u> of the deadlines listed on <u>all</u> of your syllabi, using a <u>different</u> color ink or pencil for each course. Then block off reasonable periods of social time, including trips and visits home. Finally, use your color code to mark the assigned pages of reading for each course and the weekly topics (if they are listed on the syllabus). Believe it or not, you have already begun to study!

FEBRUARY							
Week's Topics	**Sunday**	**Monday**	**Tuesday**	**Wednesday**	**Thursday**	**Friday**	**Saturday**
Ps Brain p. 104-135 Ph Plato p. 57-88 PS Congress p. 215-247 M Factoring p. 85-90	1	2 Psychology Test Drive Mark to Piano Lessons	3 Work 3-9 pm	4 Basketball Game	5 Philosophy Quiz Work 5-9 pm	6 Math Test	7
Ps Memory p. 294-337 Ph Aristotle p. 89-104 PS Judiciary p. 250-299 M Binomials p. 96-100	8	9 NO CLASSES CURRICULUM DAY Drive Mark to Piano Lessons	10 Political Science Test Work 3-9 pm	11 Psychology Paper Due Basketball Game	12 Work 5-9 pm	13 Math Test	14 Valentine's Dinner with Chris
Ps Stress p. 379-441 Ph Socrates p. 106-122 PS Executive p. 301-338 M Quadratics p. 105-110	15 Home for Mom's Birthday	16 Psychology Test Drive Mark to Piano Lessons	17 Work 3-9 pm	18 Basketball Game	19 Philosophy Quiz Work 5-9 pm	20 Math Test Joe's Party	21
Ps Learning p. 340-376 Ph Hume p. 160-189 Ps Treasury p. 356-399 M Quadratics p. 110-114	22	23 Drive Mark to Piano Lessons	24 Philosophy Paper Due Work 3-9 pm	25 Basketball Game	26 Political Science Paper Due Work 5-9 pm	27 Math Test	28 Baby-sit for Rita

Figure 3

Since studying is mental organization, this basic (and most often neglected) step in mental visualization sets the tone for all of your future efforts. Now that you can see where you

VISUALIZE YOUR TERM

are going from your *mental helicopter*, you have a great advantage over those who may try to approach the same objective *from the ground*, without *scouting the terrain* beforehand.

This also serves to identify the rhythm of activity you will establish throughout the term. If you are well organized and the course tasks are at regular intervals, you will need to expend less effort in figuring out what to do next because it is built into your monthly routine. I cannot overemphasize the value of mental rhythm, because this allows automatic prediction of tasks and frees up your mind for more important details.

Now, take a small break. Gather your textbooks together at your desk alongside your master calendar. After your break, take each one of your textbooks and flip through the pages you will cover in each course, referring to your calendar. Look at the pictures and browse the topic subheadings. You have just previewed your term, and <u>without any further work at this point</u>, your brain will unconsciously, automatically, be

PREVIEWING IS THE UNIVERSAL TIME SAVER

forming questions about what you have seen. It also will begin to create a schematic representation of the entire course, so that all further work will serve to fill in the blanks. This saves hours of time later on.

STEP #3 -- TAKE ONE WEEK AT A TIME

Then, each Sunday evening, before the beginning of the school week, take 10 minutes to browse through all of the material to be covered in that coming week, as you define and set your short-term mental goals. If you do this <u>consistently</u>, you

VISUALIZING WEEKLY GOALS IDENTIFIES PROBLEMS TO BE SOLVED

will be amazed at how much easier it is to relate to the lectures and how much more of the material presented in class you will remember after hearing it only one time. Your study time will be cut dramatically and your retention will increase as you build an unforgettable mental concept of the material.

You will find that you need far less study time to accomplish the same level of understanding because the entire picture of what is going on will be enhanced when you approach the text to read it thoroughly later. You will tend to fall asleep over your books less and less, and you will actually find yourself interested in courses you never dreamed you could enjoy.

Why? Because the brain is an amazing problem-solver. It seems to be a fact of life that whenever we can solve a problem, we feel a basic happiness at our accomplishment. We rise to a challenge and rejoice when we are successful. We are goal-oriented, organization-prone organisms. It is simply how the brain works.

MY BRAIN'S JOB IS TO ORGANIZE MY WORLD

To realize this, you only have to watch a toddler hard at work fitting an oval block into an oval hole, turning it every which way until it finally goes in. With great smiles she looks around for someone close by to share in her great success. We are all like this, and the tremendous challenge of the coming school term only goes sour when we feel mowed under by the seemingly uncontrollable demands.

Have you ever noticed that we only intensely dislike those courses that we do not feel successful in? Because we can't escape, the sense of failure is overwhelming and resentment grows as a *learned helplessness* sets in.

LACK OF SUCCESS = DISLIKE THE SUBJECT

At the same time, by previewing you are employing another tip from memory research. It is well known that distributed study yields better retention. Here you are, prepared for the school week, having already gone over the material twice! Now during your first time in class, you can begin to fill in the blanks, because you have already passed through the

PREVIEWING HELPS US REMEMBER DETAILS

initial stage of "what are you talking about?" You have gone right to the stage of organizing the details within the mental concepts you identified in the term overview and the weekly preview.

The brain organizes an overview automatically the first time material is encountered. It tries to fit it into past knowledge and experience somehow, because physiologically, information cannot be remembered any other way. If your first encounter is in class, you will spend the entire session trying to figure out the topic and the limits of the information. But, if you have already previewed the information, you know which *ballpark you are playing in* and your mind can settle down to the business of sorting facts and organizing concepts.

HOW MUCH TIME DO I NEED?

In college, most instructors plan the student workload on at least a 2:1 ratio (some courses like math require a 3:1 ratio). This means that for every hour of class time, you will be required to spend 2 study hours per week outside of class. For example, a 3 credit-hour course requires <u>at least</u> 6 hours per week of outside study (organization). Be sure to schedule that in. This is not negotiable. You cannot get around it and be successful.

When assessing your workload for the term, you must take this into consideration, or you will find yourself shortchanging your study, your family, your work or other responsibilities. It helps to add up the total weekly commitment you are making before you ever register for classes to make sure that the expectations you are putting yourself under are reasonable.

> ### REMEMBER:
> FOR <u>ALL</u> CLASSES, YOU WILL NEED TO SCHEDULE IN
> <u>AT LEAST TWO</u> HOURS OF STUDY PER WEEK
> <u>OUTSIDE</u> OF CLASS FOR <u>EVERY</u> HOUR SPENT <u>IN</u> CLASS,
> AS <u>SOON</u> AFTER CLASS AS POSSIBLE

Even within that ratio, you can increase comprehension and cut study time dramatically by previewing your texts ahead of time and viewing the topics as concepts rather than as groups of details. If you understand a concept, the details will follow automatically. It is like trying to take a huge pile of laundry to the washer. Without a laundry bag, many pieces would drop along the way, just as details get lost without a concept to hold them together.

PLANNING FOR DIFFERENT TYPES OF COURSES

There are basically three types of courses you will encounter. There are content courses, skill courses, and process courses. Each type of course requires slightly different scheduling, so you want to be aware of that from the beginning.

Content courses concentrate on learning a volume of material knowledge. These courses include history, sociology, psychology, political science, anthropology, and all other courses that focus upon <u>identifying</u>, <u>knowing</u>, and <u>understanding</u> facts, ideas and concepts. These are some of the most challenging for incoming freshmen, because of the volume of material covered so rapidly. The keys to these courses are scheduling, previewing, and conceptual thinking.

1. Keeping to a study schedule will provide control.
2. Previewing your text before you read it will give direction to your reading and decrease study time.
3. Thinking in concepts rather than in details will aid in compare-contrast exercises and cement the information as a total picture, helping you retain the material over the long term.

Skill courses concentrate on acquiring a skill, such as composition, languages, and computer skills. Any course that requires practice to achieve a grade is a skill course. Such courses require that you schedule two hours of practice time for each in-class hour, and that you keep in mind the campus lab's hours or times when you can access the required practice materials. Clear understanding of procedures and organized, regular practice are the keys.

1.   If you do not clearly understand the procedures, practice may only confuse you.

2.   Regular practice trains your mind and body to respond appropriately.

Process courses focus on learning a mental process, like math, philosophy, logic, and literature. Such courses develop a way of viewing the world or of analyzing information. Realize that you might have to spend <u>more</u> than two hours per class hour per week because they require both information input <u>and</u> mental practice. (Even though your instructor may assign a ratio of reading and homework that can be done in two hours for each class hour, you might not catch on right away.) Depending upon your past experience with similar courses, you may need more or less time to master the thinking process involved. Schedule in optional time for additional practice and thought. Conceptual thinking and practice are the keys.

1.   By thinking in organized concepts rather than in details, you have a mental picture to draw from as you solve the problems that are always the focus of such courses.

> **REMEMBER: THOUGHT TAKES TIME**

2.   By regularly practicing the thought processes you are learning, you are ensuring that you know them, and can test out at any time. **This is particularly critical in math.**

Now that you have looked at your term logically and rationally, preparing for the proper amounts of time to be spent on each of your classes, you can pretty well predict what your term will be like. With this, there comes a wave of relief as you feel like you have a grip on the near future. You have control over your situation: "I can do this." Anxiety is lessened, memory is freed, you can relax and get to work.

The next three chapters explore the "Big 3" themes of memory research: organization, timing and overlearning.

CHAPTER 2 = ORGANIZATION & MORE ORGANIZATION

Since study is organization, everything that clarifies material helps set it into memory in a usable form. Therefore, it only makes sense that successful study involves having a set of clear, specific rules to follow. That way, if we don't quite get the results we want, we can go back systematically and check on which rule we need to give more attention. There are sixteen rules that will take us through the study process. These rules are based on the data from countless hours of memory research and following them will ensure the maximum success with the minimum amount of effort. In other words, we will make the most of our precious time and resources. Remember that researchers have found that it is _what you do with the information_ that determines retention.

WHAT YOU SEE IS WHAT YOU GET
RULE #1 = GET RID OF DISTRACTIONS

Our selective attention is like a narrow doorway that only allows a single item in at a time. What we attend to is what enters through the door. It is simply a matter of priorities. One major problem in studying new information is our tendency to try and attend to more than one thing at a time. That is like two or three people trying to barge through a door together. It just

PRIORITIES DETERMINE ATTENTION

doesn't work, because when we don't prioritize consciously, our brain automatically decides which one gets in and which ones don't. We have lost conscious control. This is why distractions are so devastating to study.

Now, distractions will be different for each person because each person has different priorities. So you need to discover what prevents you, individually, from attending to course material. It may be noise, food, other people, your surroundings, an uncomfortable chair, etc. Whatever it is, minimize all distractions as much as humanly possible.

What is wrong with this picture?

> *Carla is studying for a big Anatomy test. She is slouching at the dining room table of her apartment with her books spread out. Her roommate is cooking dinner while she watches TV in the kitchen. In the living room, the stereo is pounding out rock music and a party is going on upstairs. She reads a paragraph over four times and closes her book, frustrated. She tells her roommate, "I guess I must be stupid or something. I just can't seem to understand this stuff."*

There is nothing wrong with Carla. She may feel frustrated, but she is perfectly normal. Because her senses are taking in so much information at once, her capacity to attend to her Anatomy class is blocked by all of the external interference. All she needs to do is find or create a quiet place to work, choose a time when not so much is going on around her, turn off the stereo, or do <u>whatever is needed</u> for her attention to be focused on Anatomy at that time.

If you don't minimize your distractions and interruptions, you will never give yourself a chance to attend to your course material. Remember, it isn't necessary to have hours and hours that are quiet and uninterrupted. Simply establish a place where you can concentrate completely for an average of 20 minutes at a time.

DO IT RIGHT THE FIRST TIME
RULE #2 = ALWAYS READ WITH PENCIL AND PAPER, TAKING NOTES

Research has discovered that students who take notes as they read textbook material for the first time recall it far better later on. Somehow, the exercise of organizing as soon as we contact information is one of the most powerful techniques to raise grades and decrease overall study time. Why?

TAKE NOTES AS YOU READ

Because we are giving our brains presorted, distinct memory images to remember, either as pictures, outlines or compare-contrast charts of our own design.

We cannot expect our brain to remember the information if all we do is read it. That is physiologically impossible because new information must be stored in relation to previous input. Even understanding a sentence in the textbook requires a frame of reference, because we must know what the words mean.

The first time we read anything, our brains are trying to relate it to something we already know, as we establish that frame of reference. That's why we need to go back and clarify information after a first reading. It's like moving into a new home and throwing everything into a pile to be sorted out later.

PUT INFORMATION INTO CORRECT ORDER RIGHT AWAY

How much more time and order efficient we will be if we put every new load into its proper place as soon as we bring it in. This also contributes to distinctiveness because you have never encoded the information in any other (disorganized) form. It makes perfect sense to take notes as we read a chapter the first time.

Another enemy of organization occurs automatically as our selective attention shifts to new situations and different information enters through the door in quick succession, so to make the most of what we hear or read, we need to observe the next rule.

DON'T CONFUSE ME
RULE #3 = CREATE CLEAR BREAKS BETWEEN SUBJECTS

Dale is sitting in Philosophy class and thinking that he will never forget what Prof. Thesis just said. When class ends, he gets up and walks across campus to his English Literature class. After that session, he sits down to lunch and tries to remember what both teachers were talking about.

Shaking his head in frustration, he closes his books and gives up. Even this little amount of interference makes it difficult for him to recall what Prof. T said. Because his thoughts from that class were not clarified, he had a hard time concentrating on the second class lecture, AND DID NOT REMEMBER EITHER ONE SUCCESSFULLY.

As you have probably observed, it takes thoughtful effort (including imagining yourself back in that classroom) to distinguish between what was said in each class, especially if they involve similar information, like two different languages or Psychology and Sociology. Why? Because of something memory researchers call *proactive* and *retroactive interference*.

Pro means *ahead*, so proactive interference simply means that what you have learned before interferes with new learning. In the same way, *retro* means *backward*, so retroactive interference means that what you learn afterward interferes with remembering previously learned material. It is a well-documented phenomenon.

The answer to this dilemma is to schedule college classes with breaks in between for immediate review of class notes IF AT ALL POSSIBLE. Now, due to scheduling limitations, this may be highly

REVIEW & PREVIEW BETWEEN CLASSES

unrealistic, but it is the best-case scenario. If this is unavoidable (as it often is), you must make an effort to distinguish between the two classes as much as you can.

You may use different colored papers or inks to take notes

KEEP CLASSES DISTINCT FROM EACH OTHER

in each class, or use different notebooks. Anything you can do to distinguish between the classes and their respective material will help greatly. The most important thing is to make a conscious effort at differentiating the material.

When you study later, work with your courses one at a time, with at least 5 minutes in between where you get a snack, stretch, take a walk, rest your eyes, wash dishes, work at a menial job, or whatever. While you are taking your break, your marvelous brain keeps on working, putting all of the new information into order for you. Instead of being a time of mental rest, it is really a time

BREAKS ALLOW YOUR BRAIN TO SORT INFORMATION

to sort through and organize what has just entered through the door. Caution: don't watch TV or put in any new information from a different source during these breaks. Let your brain organize in peace.

Through all of memory research, there is a single principle that isolates the most basic requirement for 100% recall.

THE MAGIC WORD: DISTINCTIVENESS
RULE #4 = NOTICE THE DIFFERENCES BETWEEN TERMS & IDEAS

By making the pieces of information different, it is easy to distinguish between them while thinking about the topic and to remember them come test time when you need to demonstrate that you have mastered the material. In order for something to be distinct, it must be clear. Clarity is critical for memory. **Anything not distinct (unclear) is not remembered.** Period. That is why this rule is so powerful.

TO REMEMBER SOMETHING, IT MUST BE CLEAR

The whole process of study only works when it produces distinctiveness, beginning with simple, basic grouping of similar material. Making information cues clear and distinct produces virtually perfect recall in research subjects, particularly when added to understanding the relationships between the cues. In other words, grouping similar information together and understanding the difference between the groups equals perfect recall.

DISTINCTIVENESS = PERFECT RECALL

> *Cody sat at his desk, puzzled. He read the essay test question over three times. He knew he had read something about the dynasties in ancient China, but he couldn't remember their prominent characteristics or how they related together. If his teacher had simply asked names and dates, he was all right, because he had memorized those, but not their significance. How was he supposed to know all of this?*

Needless to say, Cody is not alone. We have all felt that sense of hopelessness whenever the test questions are not in exactly the same form as the textbook or our notes. But this is simply the instructor's way of seeing if you KNOW what the information means, instead of just parroting back bare trivia.

Yes, this is fair. This is college level thinking, and we can never succeed at answering such questions unless we learn to clarify the information so that we understand concepts and the relationships between them.

This differentiation can be done in many ways, but always works best when done while you are reading the material the very first time. Your brain begins that mental picture as soon as you first encounter the information, so

COLLEGE LEVEL THINKING = UNDERSTANDING CONCEPTS & RELATIONSHIPS

always read your texts with pencil and paper, taking notes and drawing diagrams of what it is saying.

Gary, the engineer, may make flow charts or hierarchies of the information. Dina, the art student, may draw pictures or color-code the main concepts as she underlines her text and class notes. Pete, the English major, likes to make charts of similar words or ideas as he organizes them into categories.

Frank, the premed student, tries to recreate the text author's outline on his own.

One simple way to differentiate is to draw a line down the middle of a page and collect data about two different terms or ideas on opposite sides of the page. As you differentiate, general principles of relationship will begin to emerge and you will find yourself grouping facts and ideas.

	CLASSICAL CONDITIONING	OPERANT CONDITIONING
Behavior:	PASSIVE	ACTIVE
Controlling Stimulus (i.e. Food) Comes:	BEFORE	AFTER
Generalization?	YES	YES
Discrimination?	YES	YES
Extinction?	YES	YES

Figure 4

I cannot emphasize enough that each person relates to material differently. A few years back, I had a student who had the top score nationally on a military electronics test. Obviously, he was highly intelligent, but he could not relate to a standard outline format. His test scores improved and his frustration level declined after I showed him how to interpret the lecture notes and text organization as a hierarchy (like an electronics diagram--Figure 5), the way he naturally related to information. Spatially gifted students will benefit from this technique. Add a color code to the boxes and you have a powerful pictorial representation of large amounts of material at a glance.

There is nothing special about traditional outlines. They are simply one way to communicate relationship between ideas, and any alternative method will do just as well.

SOCIOLOGY 101

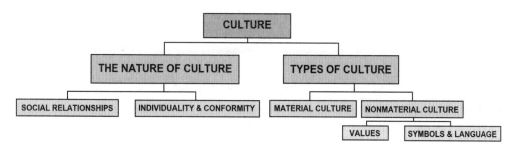

Figure 5

CHUNK IT ALL TOGETHER
RULE #5 = GROUP BOOK & LECTURE NOTES TOGETHER BY TOPIC

Oh yes! I understand this subject quite well. I read it over twice and it really makes sense. But this is only the beginning of the process. If you have only read the material, you have not yet begun to study. For many students, this is shocking news.

Eva read her notes over and over before her Political Science test and was relaxed and happy. She was confident because she understood all of the material. As the tests were passed out and she looked at the page, her heart stopped. She didn't know most of the questions!

> *She had never thought through the material in this way. It was as if the instructor had passed out a test for the wrong class. Anxiety rose, memory faded and she ended up bombing it royally.*

Eva never thought about the information in any other way than the face value of her notes. She had read her text and notes, but she had never grouped her notes together for meaning or integrated them with the textbook information. Further, she had not asked what type of questions would be on the test and had not directed her study accordingly. So, it really threw a wrench in the works when the instructor changed the wording from exactly what she had read. Just recognizing terms or remembering bare facts is not enough when it comes to testing time, especially in college. (Remember, this shift in the required level of comprehension is one of the main differences between high school and college.)

**COLLEGE LEVEL STUDY =
A CHANGE FROM FACTS TO COMPREHENSION
&
PASSIVE TO ACTIVE THOUGHT**

To fix this, we first need to put our minds to work and see which information relates together. If we understand the material, this is really a very simple task, one that takes a minimum of effort, but it is this one, powerful first step that transforms us from mere passive consumers of textbook data into active thinkers. This one small catalyst charges up our batteries and thrusts us deep into the realm of real study. We have begun climbing the stairway to academic success.

Not only does grouping like this aid in understanding, but it also allows us to remember bits of information as larger *chunks*. A *chunk* is any meaningful unit of information, and is based upon our past experience with similar material. So, as we group

WE REMEMBER *CHUNKS* OF INFORMATION

new information by how it fits together, we automatically multiply our capacity to remember more material because we are sorting it by meaning.

Researchers have found that organizing material at the time when we first encounter it greatly enhances our recall ability. Not only does it clarify the information, but grouping automatically files facts and ideas away by topic or meaning, to be remembered as a unit. Instead of

ORGANIZE MATERIAL THE <u>FIRST</u> TIME YOU SEE IT

having to remember isolated facts, we are able to access many facts and relationships by recalling one simple category. In fact, research has shown that the strongest relationship between study time and test scores was when study time was spent organizing course content. (Remember what we noticed about previewing material and taking book notes as you read?)

For example, it is easy to read that Henry VIII had six wives and everybody knows this basic fact. But, group the six different ladies with the dates of their marriage, their countries of birth, their religions and the years of his reign, and a fascinating picture of Henry's political and religious life begins to emerge. By grouping for meaning, you can think through different questions based on that information and you can build further idea schemas on that base of facts. Not only that, but by grouping for meaning, the trivial dates and facts fall into place as you recall the relationships and your memory for the supporting details is almost automatic.

Zack went to Sociology class on Monday. That afternoon, he sat at his desk and took notes as he read the portions of his text covering the same material. As he put his book and lecture notes together, he created a more complete picture of the topic. Tuesday, although he didn't have class, he reviewed all of his notes. After class Wednesday he repeated the process of merging text and lecture and Thursday he reviewed all notes to date. By repeating this process daily over the two-week period between exams, he ended up with a complete, clear mental picture of the topic and was able to recall facts, names, dates, and other necessary information well enough to answer all of the questions on his test. He had studied successfully.

When you do this, it is actually hard to stop your mind from asking questions or arguing with the text. You are organizing, you are chunking, you are sorting and storing information by category. You are hooked. In fact, I challenge you to group the items together and not automatically make it your own.

IT'S MINE
RULE #6 = MAKE YOUR OWN COMPARE & CONTRAST CHARTS

Marla likes to draw a line down the middle of a page and make a compare-and-contrast chart (see Figure 4). As she takes the information out of the text, she puts it together with her notes from lecture. She likes to group the information in each column by similarities and differences. When she comes to a question she has, she circles it in pencil, to be erased when she finds the answer.

As we think about <u>relationships</u> and the <u>attributes</u> that make each group of information different, we are deeply into the heart of *study*. Not only are we gaining understanding of the material, but this information is being burned deep into our memories by all of the complex

NOTICE SIMILARITIES & DIFFERENCES

mental activity we are generating. Research has shown repeatedly that when students note the differences, similarities and relationships between information, they experience both the greatest gains in test performance and protection against forgetting over time.

Many studies have addressed recall of textbook information and have all shown that the key is organization and interrelation of ideas. In fact, researchers have found that the best conditions for recall were simultaneously organizing by relationships and clearly separating groups of facts. Organization by relationship emphasizes similarities and making items specific emphasizes differences. In other words, *compare and contrast*.

One of the most powerful features of this technique is that you generate your own categories for sorting. By noticing the differences and similarities between ideas, people, time periods, etc., an original concept begins to form, a schema, a single picture of the course material that is yours alone. When experimental subjects generate their own categories, they show

CREATE YOUR OWN CATEGORIES

far better recall than if the experimenter chooses them. Self-generating groups and ideas increases the mental processing of relationships, which increases memory.

Anything that differentiates the concepts and details requires your brain to think the material through, and the more you *process* the information in different ways, the more solid your memory will be at test time.

THE POWER OF "WHY?"
RULE #7 = LOOK UP INFORMATION YOU ARE NOT SURE ABOUT

Another very effective method is to ask yourself "why" questions. It is called *elaborative interrogation* and it is one of the most successful techniques for setting something into memory. (By the way, this is the whole rationale behind creating and using workbooks and study guides.)

Self-questioning to determine omitted information not only provides a focus for selective attention, but it also produces motivation, direction, and momentum as it propels you forward into new *aha* experiences and the entire subject-picture falls into place for you.

Research has shown that students who use "why" questions showed greater memory for new subject matter. One major reason for this was the students' relating the new information to what they already knew and understood. It seemed to promote better integration of the material because

> **"WHY?" QUESTIONS LINK NEW MATERIAL TO EXISTING KNOWLEDGE**

they had to draw from prior knowledge and develop stronger interconnections among facts. Also, the information has an immediate, practical purpose (to answer a question). Because our minds are geared to solving problems, they become quite satisfied when all questions are answered. In this way, it serves as a reward.

> **A PICTURE IS WORTH.....**
> *RULE #8 = DRAW & COLOR CODE PICTURES, CHARTS & DIAGRAMS*

Research records dramatic use of pictures in tests of item recovery. It has long been noted that, "A picture is worth a thousand words." This is logical, since

1.   organization consists of a mental picture,

2.   creating mental pictures of the material is the goal of study, and

3.   the process is speeded up dramatically when we see or create a picture in the first place.

Some researchers even view our short-term memory as a

work area where we bring pictures back to mind in order to apply them to new situations (they call it a *visuo-spatial scratch pad*). To encode actual images (pictures) facilitates this process and enables us to *chunk* information for storage more efficiently.

> *Marty made charts of everything. He found it especially helpful to color code his charts and draw pictures of whatever he found confusing. When he read his texts, he looked at the pictures first to get the focus of the chapter before he ever began to read the content. Just like research has shown us, Marty recalled the information far better on all of his tests when he related to pictures than when he only relied on his notes and the written text.*

I'VE NEVER SEEN THIS STUFF BEFORE
RULE #9 = STUDY FOR THE TYPE OF TEST YOU WILL TAKE

Remember that to recall information, it must first be encoded, and encoding includes the WAY it is to be recalled. Here is where knowing what <u>kind</u> of testing your instructor uses is of great benefit. He/she will usually tell you what form the test will be in, whether multiple choice, essay, true-false, etc. You must realize that EACH TYPE OF TEST REQUIRES A DIFFERENT EMPHASIS IN ENCODING. Allow me to explain.

Suppose you are going to have a multiple-choice test. You will look at the material from the viewpoint of term definitions, basic relationship, and important principles. Depending upon the course material and the textbook, definitions may be the focus, or more complex understanding of names or concepts may be what you are tested on. There are both *data based* and *concept based* multiple-choice tests. (*Data based* questions test on definitions and bare facts, whereas *concept based*

DIFFERENT TYPES OF TESTS REQUIRE DIFFERENT TYPES OF ENCODING

questions test on ideas, requiring thought integration and identification of principles.)

Whatever the emphasis, make sure that same emphasis is the base and focus of your mental organization (study), and *that you are able to explain the course material to someone else from that standpoint.*

SCORES ARE HIGH WHEN STUDY CUES = TEST CUES

Researchers have found that the maximum success at retrieval (exams) happens when students encode the information in the exact same form as the test questions. In fact, the closer the test questions are to the form in which the students have encoded the information, the better their scores, and changing the recall cues results in a higher percentage of errors.

This even applies to the physical location in which the student studies and the mood he/she is in. When we study, our entire context is encoded together as a package along with the material. The closer the entire

EVEN LOCATION & MOOD ARE IMPORTANT

package of test cues is to the study situation, the easier it is to test and the better our score. Some researchers view our learning environment as a set of *memory landmarks* that guide us through a test.

Eddy is determined not to let the same thing happen twice. The last test he took in Anthropology was a disaster. He studied for hours and nearly failed the test because he had studied only general concepts and Prof. Piltdown had tested on glossary definitions. This time he was prepared.

First, he checked with Prof. P to find out if the test format was similar to the last one. It was. Okay, now Eddy knew he was studying for a multiple choice, terminology test. So he laid out all of the key terms in the material covered by the test and worked on understanding them and how they basically related together. Even if Prof. P threw in any matching questions, he was ready.

Ask. Very few instructors will hesitate to tell students what TYPE of test they will be giving. Some teachers will even provide library access to some of their old tests as study models. Use this information to focus your study efforts. As your target differs, so does your strategy.

CHAPTER 3 = IT'S ALL IN THE TIMING

How would you like to cut your required study time by 10% to 15%? Well, I'll let you in on a little secret. It is called timing, and making the most of timing can save you a bundle of headaches, not to mention valuable hours. You can have the strongest swing in the major leagues, but if your timing is off, you never hit the ball.

TIMING IS CRITICAL

How does this apply to study? The next four rules explain how timing your study efforts correctly can multiply the results exponentially...and why.

ONE MORE TIME
RULE #10 = READ & REVIEW IMMEDIATELY AFTER CLASS

No matter how successful you are at separating your classes from one another, review the class notes IMMEDIATELY after that class. Do not wait. Instead of talking to the person next to you or staring at the ceiling while you are waiting for the next class period to start, read over your notes from the last class. Then put them away and pick up the text for your upcoming class. Flip through the pages of the chapter to be covered in the next hour and look at the pictures and sub-topics once more. Then close the book and get ready for lecture. This allows you to separate the information consciously, deliberately, clearly, instead of putting it all in the pot and sorting through it later, when things have been

TO SEPARATE INFORMATION CONSCIOUSLY:
REVIEW CLASS #1
+
PREVIEW CLASS #2

muddled together. It helps establish conscious control of your efforts. (And you know what control does for confidence.)

> **CONTROL CREATES CONFIDENCE**

There is also a physical reason for this in how the brain works. In the area that relays memories to their storage places, there are certain cells that change permanently to allow easier recall when they are stimulated successively in the same way.

This same principle seems to apply to reviewing information as soon as possible after class. It is easier to recall information that has been repeated at least once immediately after the first encounter. If we students review material immediately after it is first presented, we will remember it much better than if we go over it at a later time. There is less in the way, and it is clearer and easier to recall. We may even remember parts of the class session that we had not recorded in our notes and we can elaborate on them, giving us a more complete picture.

> **TO LAY DOWN A MEMORY, GO OVER IT TWICE, IMMEDIATELY**

The first time we encounter new material, it is processed shallowly and is subject to easy decay. It can be altered by the interference of other classes or even by conversations or experiences with friends that occur before you can go over the material the second time to *lay down the memory*.

Reviewing the information immediately after hearing it for the first time makes your encoding for the information stronger, like tracing over a pencil line twice makes it darker and easier to read. In any case, DO NOT WAIT to review your notes. Also, do your required course work AS SOON AS POSSIBLE after it is first presented (this is a second reason why procrastination kills memory --Appendix II). Here are a few suggestions:

1. *Follow up your lecture time with a quick review of your notes.*

2. *Rewrite your notes, if possible, adding other information you recall.*

3. *Read text material related to the lecture topic as soon as possible after class.*

4. *Discuss the material with someone else.*

5. *Put your own questions about the material into words.*

6. *Write your questions down to be answered later. They will be a study guide for you.*

7. *Ask any unanswered questions you have before the test. Do not go into a test unclear on any point. (Reduce the stress of uncertainty.)*

Investing an identical amount of time in study on the same topic yields twice the results if it is done at the beginning of the 1 or 2 week period rather than at the end. An additional benefit is that you have ample time to review repeatedly before your test.

Donna breathed a sigh of relief and closed her notebook at the end of class. Whew! That was finally over! Professor Boredom really lived up to his name today. As she crowded out of the room, she couldn't wait to get to the SUB and get some lunch, talk to her boyfriend, and relax. Later that evening, she decided to go to the Campus Comedy Club with her roommate instead of studying, and it wasn't until the weekend that she even cracked open the text for that class.

Sunday night, as she opened the text to read the chapter for the past week, she thought, "Oh, my! This doesn't look familiar at all. How does this fit in to what Prof. Boredom was saying? What _was_ he saying, anyway? Looking at her notes for that day, she came to two unfinished sentences she had scribbled and some single words next to a partial outline. In the margins she had noted that an assignment was due next week and she remembered thinking, "That's so obvious. I won't forget that." So she hadn't written it down. Oh boy!

In a panic, Donna tried to phone the girl who sat next to her to get the assignment and to find out what those sentences could have been, but she didn't have her number. She called a mutual friend to get it. Her friend wasn't home, so she tried two others without success. Finally, she got hold of a guy's number who also had that class. 45 minutes later she settled down to study, hopeful that the information given her by the fourth person she called was accurate. No, that person hadn't written down those same sentences in that way and no, he wasn't sure of the assignment, either.

Not only did Donna waste nearly one precious hour of prime thinking time and manage to short-circuit her study plans, but she added a good dose of memory-robbing anxiety to the pot. All because she didn't go over her notes immediately, while they were fresh in her mind and she could remember easily what Prof. B had said about the course material and the assignment.

By all means, read the corresponding text material as soon as possible after class and notice how your class notes fit in. Then you will get the same picture of the material that your instructor has. (And guess who makes up the tests.)

Finally, once you *dump the information into the hopper,* your brain works to digest it automatically, much like your stomach digests food. It is an automatic process. Even if you just review your notes once before leaving for work or a sports event, you allow your brain to chew on the problem while you are gone. Make the best use of your brain's natural problem solving capacity. You will spend less time understanding the material once you return to it.

THE BRAIN AUTOMATICALLY CHEWS WHAT YOU FEED IT

You may have noticed that so far, we haven't mentioned how much and how often to go over information. Even though repetition doesn't ensure recall, it can still assist in the process if it is done correctly, with organization and distinctiveness as the focus. The next rule gives us some guidelines as to how much and how often.

BITS & PIECES
RULE #11 = STUDY ONE SECTION AT A TIME & KEEP IT SHORT

"Why only one section at a time? And why not keep reading until I have finished the entire assignment?" This is the common reaction to this rule, which is based upon a long-established finding in memory research called the *serial position effect.* Somehow, we remember most easily the first and last elements that we read. We may use this as an effective tool by working with less material at a time for shorter periods, in order to eliminate what would otherwise be in the middle of a long study session.

Using this principle, we cover an amount of material small enough that we can recall the entire piece easily. As we sort information and notice differences and similarities, this small group of text material becomes a *chunk* of information, stored and recalled as a unit or concept which is linked together by association, meaning and organization. Then we can begin the next block and repeat the process.

> **REHEARSAL**
> **+**
> **ORGANIZATION =**
> **RECALL**

Everyone knows that repetition (rehearsal) of material makes it easier for us to recall it. There is a direct relationship between how often we rehearse and how fast and completely we can recall it, but we can still review repeatedly with only limited success if we are only *reading* the text and notes. What is missing? Organization. This is the critical factor in successful recall.

It is not surprising that repetition, this most popular memory technique, has a neurological basis. When nerve cells are stimulated, they grow new branching connections between them. The nerve pathways become both more closely interconnected and increasingly sensitive with increased use, requiring less stimulation to fire again.

So, the best tactic is to schedule your study time in <u>no more</u> than 1 hour blocks (an average of 20 minutes is perfect). Read one subheading or section of your text and the lecture notes that pertain to that section. Write down the highlights IN

YOUR OWN WORDS. Take a short break. A solitary, relaxation break is best. No TV. No intense conversation. That would be like recording over a video tape. Just walk the dog, do the dishes, or play with the kids. At least 5 minutes later go back and tackle the next

PROFITABLE STUDY SESSIONS = 20 TO 60 MINUTES MAXIMUM

section. During that time, your brain will have assimilated and begun to work on organizing the information automatically.

Since the textbook author wrote from a picture outline in his/her head and since your goal is to reconstruct that same picture outline, encoding in sections, with understanding and elaboration, makes 100% sense.

This is a great help for parents who are interrupted by children needing attention, or workers who can study a section before they drive

RECREATE THE AUTHOR'S MENTAL PICTURE

to work or on coffee and lunch breaks from mentally undemanding labor. Even though no intervening activity is best, merely grouping the information together the first time you encounter it and separating study sessions by some type of break will help you tremendously later on. Contrary to common thinking, long study stretches are not the best way to approach material.

Noreen was scared to take Geography 101. She heard it was a lot of reading and she knew that she had to work evenings at the hospital. How could she do it? She tried reading one chapter section just before she left for work, another section at her first break, and a third one at her lunch break. When she got home, she read the last section and went to bed. Then, the next morning, she skimmed over what she had read and finished the few pages left in the chapter before class.

Not only was she ready to understand the lecture material, but she had a clear mental picture of the subject. She remembered the lectures better, so she had to spend less time making sense of her notes and she could ace the test. She had not spent very much time at each session, but during the time she was driving and working, her brain was working, too!

CLIMB IN THE *MEMORY WINDOW* RULE #12 = REVIEW YOUR TEXT AND LECTURE NOTES <u>DAILY</u>

Why do I need to review my notes daily if I have read the text once at the beginning of the week? Because the task of acquiring new memories occurs in stages, and it is extremely important to allow time between reviews of the same material. There is evidence that after the first time we go over new information, the brain continues to process it, inter-relating it with other items and promoting elaboration. You might say that new information is processed automatically after it is first encountered. Then, allowing time between study sessions enables the brain to lay down *memory traces* which are strengthened by repetition and elaboration (teaching material to others and/or asking "Why?" questions).

Like I mentioned earlier, once you put the information *in the mental hopper*, you need time to allow your brain to *chew* the *bite* you have just *fed* it. Your brain will continue to process the information regardless of what you do. Then, if you take just 15 minutes daily to review your text & class notes, you will create a memory pattern you

> **IT TAKES TIME TO THINK**

cannot forget. In this way, you are making the most of your valuable time.

It takes time to think. It takes the brain time to lay down complex memories. Research has revealed an optimum

> **IT TAKES THE BRAIN AT LEAST 2 DAYS TO PROCESS NEW INFORMATION**

window of time when new information is processed: between 2 days and 2 weeks. Here is another powerful reason for not *cramming*, for doing your course work immediately after the

corresponding class session and for allowing at least 2 days between the time you first encode and retrieve (test out on) any new material.

This powerful phenomenon of ongoing storage occurs most strongly during REM (dream) sleep. Therefore, observe Rule #13.

> **JUST SLEEP ON IT**
> *RULE #13 = GET A GOOD NIGHT'S SLEEP AFTER STUDY*

We can all remember times when we have dreamt vividly about what we have just studied, or times when we have awakened in the morning with the answer to a thorny problem we were working on the night before. This phenomenon is so common that one theory of dreaming labels it as a mental state of problem solving.

Research has proven that REM (Rapid Eye Movement) sleep, the time when we dream vividly, is the time when new memories are laid down into permanent storage and is <u>required</u> for complete and accurate retention of studied material. Because of this inescapable, powerful fact, NEVER deprive yourself of sleep in an attempt to learn new information within a short period of time immediately before a test situation (*cramming*, or *all-nighters*). It simply doesn't work. You end up overtired, frustrated and anxious. (And that adrenaline will short-circuit your recall of whatever memory you <u>do</u> have.)

> **CRAMMING NEVER WORKS**

For the maximum retention of information, be sure you have regular sleep periods following study sessions and allow at least 2 days to process new information before taking a test. This means pacing yourself to allow plenty of time for reviewing and storing the memories as part of your mental repertoire. This is another reason why procrastination kills memory.

> **LET THE MEMORIES BECOME PART OF YOUR MENTAL REPERTOIRE**

CHAPTER 4 = OVERLEARNING ENSURES RETENTION

A common student mistake is to stop working with material once it is understood. Research has shown that the more you rehearse material you already know, the longer you will remember it. This extra practice is called overlearning, and it increases both how deeply you understand the information and how long you remember it.

There are two aspects to this: first, make the information personally meaningful and second, teach it to someone else.

CLAIMING THE TERRITORY
RULE #14 = RELATE THE INFORMATION TO YOUR LIFE

The key to long-term memory is meaning, and personal meaning is even more powerful when it comes to recall. Research has revealed repeatedly that there is a close relationship between personal significance and recall. We remember important phone numbers, dates and times. Our brains only retain material that

WE ONLY REMEMBER WHAT IS IMPORTANT TO US

is meaningful to us. Otherwise, we would be on continuous sensory overload, as we remembered every trivial event in our lives. This is one reason why our brain needs to cast off low priority memories. It cleans house daily.

To recall course material over the long term, make it personally meaningful to you. The easiest and most powerful technique I know of is to:

TELL IT TO THE CAT
RULE #15 = EXPLAIN THE INFORMATION TO SOMEONE ELSE

In explaining course material to someone else, you quickly find out what you do not understand, and this sends you back to the text and notes to research and rethink what it means.

If you can actually <u>teach</u> it to someone so that they can understand it, you know it. This also allows you to look at the material in a different way than just once-over reading and surface comprehension. When you understand the complete picture, you can use it in more practical situations, like essay tests.

In fact, there is no more powerful form of elaboration than to verbally explain information. The mental process involved in such a complex task stores memories in areas for hearing, language, concept development, organization and vocalization. By this process, you are able to use your entire brain system as it focuses on a single topic, noting both facts and relationships. This is particularly helpful if you suffer from test anxiety, since it is easier to recall information stored in multiple brain areas.

STORE INFORMATION IN DIFFERENT PARTS OF YOUR BRAIN

When tutors in college courses were tested four months later on their subject, they had far better recall than the students they tutored. If you want to really learn a subject, just teach it.

Also, teaching it to someone else allows you to interact with a living, breathing human who can tell you if you make

TO TEACH IT IS TO KNOW IT

sense or not. It challenges you, even <u>requires</u> you, to mentally organize the facts in a simple, basic form. And what is the goal of course work? ..... Right!
Transfer of an organized mental picture from instructor to student. If you have the correct, clear mental picture, then you have the basis of the entire course.

Grab a friend. Any friend. Sit him (or her) down with the offer (bribe) of a cup of coffee, lunch, or the promise of a game of pool. Then explain everything you know about your course material. Ask your friend if it makes sense and write down all of the questions that come up. This will help you identify areas where you may not be clear. Then, go back to your text and notes, find the answers to those questions and explain it again.

With dialogue you should be able to:
1. **organize the course material mentally**
2. **discover / identify areas of uncertainty**
3. **pinpoint critical data and find answers to specific key questions**
4. **refine your thinking**
5. **make the information "yours"**

Ben saw his friend, Melissa, in the SUB. "Hey, do you have a few minutes? I'd like to run something by you to see if it makes sense." Over the next half hour, Ben was able to discover what he still needed to find out about his Economics chapter when he couldn't explain it clearly. Melissa was happy to help, and she learned something about Economics, which she has to take next year.

There is a final rule that ensures our test-readiness. It is to practice test-taking.

> ## SLOGGING THROUGH MUD?
> ### RULE #16 = MAKE UP A PRACTICE TEST AND SWAP WITH A BUDDY

Players practice their sport in a gym, on the field or court, so why not practice test taking? It is quite difficult to go into any activity *cold*. When we do test out without practice, it feels like we are slogging through a field of heavy mental mud. How would you like to play in a championship basketball game after only practicing in an open field, not on a marked, hardwood gym floor? You need the same type of practice conditions that you expect at test time. Practice makes perfect!

So, make up a test of your own in the exact format your instructor will give you. When your study partner also makes up a test and you swap, take each others' tests, correct them and discuss your answers, you will be far more prepared and assured that you know the information. This mental shift from passive to active thought puts you in the driver's seat. You are viewing the information in a totally different way, with mastery and confidence. As you identify gaps in your understanding and seek out the answers, you increase your knowledge base and decrease test anxiety. You know the material thoroughly because you have made it your own.

To practice test taking may be a new idea for you. Since there is so much at stake, it only makes sense that we should take test practice quite seriously. Such an important subject requires its own chapter, so let's take a concentrated look at testing.

CHAPTER 5 = THE TASK OF TESTING

You have found out exactly how Prof. Knowmore is going to test you. He will use one of the following formats: essay, multiple choice, matching, true-false, short answer, or fill-ins.

Although not all test formats require the deepest of the three levels of memory (Figure 6), the deepest level is always the ultimate goal to reach, since that is where you can retrieve all of the information you have encoded at any time and in any form you need it. I call this the Level of Practical Use. Other types of tests can be taken from lesser levels of processing with moderate degrees of success, but it is always best to aim for Level III.

> **DIFFERENT TYPES OF TESTS NEED DIFFERENT LEVELS OF MEMORY**

SUMMARY OF MEMORY LEVELS, ENTRY KEYS & TESTING REQUIREMENTS

	ENCODING	STORAGE	RETRIEVAL
LEVEL I:	Read Text & Notes	Superficial	Superficial Cues
ENTRY: Selective Attention _MAXIMUM TESTING LEVEL:_ Recognition (Key-Word Multiple Choice)			
LEVEL II:	Understanding & Elaboration	Comprehensive	Comprehensive Cues
ENTRY: Meaning _MAXIMUM TESTING LEVEL:_ Comprehension (Concept-Based Multiple Choice, Matching, True-False, Fill-in, Short Answer)			
LEVEL III:	Personal Organization	Integrated With Life Expereinces	Active Use Cues
ENTRY: Attachment to Personal Experience _MAXIMUM TESTING LEVEL:_ Application (Essay)			

Figure 6

The chart above shows the three levels of memory and the levels of depth each type of testing requires. Selective attention is the entrance to memory, but there are three levels of depth involved. How deep and therefore how permanent your memory for course material will be depends upon HOW you encode and work with the information that comes in through selective attention.

If you only read the material and you are just able to recognize the ideas or terms, the best you can do well on are data-based multiple-choice questions that ask about terminology. You are very limited. This is because your depth of encoding is at a superficial level, retrieved by superficial cues, such as what a word looks like. Essays are out of the question. Forget even scoring well on matching or multiple-choice questions that are based on conceptual understanding. Even if a good dose of text anxiety doesn't overrun and destroy this superficial encoding, you won't reach academic success by just understanding terminology.

TARGET THE LEVEL OF DEPTH YOU NEED FOR YOUR TEST

Once you have paid attention to information (selective attention), material must be understood to reach the second level of depth. Meaning is the entry to this level and organization will help you to elaborate on the material, enriching your knowledge and storing it in your memory more permanently.

NO MEANING = NO MEMORY

It MUST have meaning to you or it remains superficial. (Even professional memory experts who memorize long lists of numbers or words rely on giving them some sort of meaning or relationship in order to recall them.)

Once you understand and elaborate on the material, tying it to other pieces of information, comparing, contrasting and noting distinctions between ideas, you are able to tackle concept-based multiple choice, true-false, matching, fill-ins, and other types of advanced test questions quite handily. The only type of question for which you are not yet fully prepared is a quality essay.

To arrive at the memory depth necessary for a superior quality essay product (as well as to ace all other types of questions, no matter how difficult the reasoning that is required)

> **ESSAYS REQUIRE THE MAXIMUM DEPTH**

it must be USEFUL to you in your everyday life. If it is, you will never forget it. For it to be useful, you must elaborate the material so that it becomes part of your complete understanding of the world. How is this accomplished?

As we have mentioned before, one primary way of

> **IF YOUCAN TEACH IT, IT'S _YOURS_**

making it your own is to teach it to somebody else. Somehow, when you have to explain it, course material becomes richer as you interact with it to understand, organize and explain it to others. I cannot emphasize this enough, because this is the supreme test of successful study. If you can teach it, you know it and it is yours forever.

PRECISE TESTING STRATEGIES

Let's talk about some precise strategies for taking different types of tests. Often, acing an essay test seems to be an elusive mystery. Here is a foolproof way to study for one.

ESSAY: Suppose you have an essay test. You know that essays are written in class and that you are expected to

1. address the question, and

2. be organized.

Let me give you a hint. ANYTHING you can do that will help the instructor clarify and understand your answer will result in a higher score. No kidding. Research has shown that student written work is penalized for <u>anything</u> that comes in the way of communication between student and teacher.

So, BE CLEAR. And in order to be clear, you must be organized. Even as in studying, distinctiveness is the key to a good essay exam grade. Clarity is essential for both input and output.

To prepare for an essay test,

1. **Go over your course material and choose about 5 possible questions the instructor might ask. (There are only so many major themes in a chapter that the instructor can address in class in 2 or 3 weeks.) You will usually get a big hint about what is considered important by the topics covered in lectures.**

2. **Prepare a brief, 3-point outline for each topic, with at least 2 sub-points each (3 sub-points is better).**

3. **Find and note details, such as names, dates, etc., to support each of your statements. Add these to your outline.**

> 4. **Talk your outlines over with a friend.**
>
> 5. **Practice writing your points out without looking at your notes.**

After this, you should be able to answer any question on that topic, because just about any question your teacher will ask can be directed to the data you have already researched. After all, you have studied the entire body of material thoroughly as you thought out your outlines. Also, you have practiced organizing the information and have facts ready to support your conclusions. You really do know the topic <u>inside and out</u> after all of that preparation.

Remember, there are 3 requirements for a quality essay:

1. ***Answer every part of the question clearly and systematically.*** Your instructor has a mental scoring map of what parts are worth how many points.

> *"Compare and contrast the philosophy of Plato with that of Aristotle on the source of human knowledge."*
> *This question has 4 parts:*
>
> *compare = similarities   Plato's philosophy*
> *contrast = differences   Aristotle's philosophy*
>
> *Each part will be worth a certain number of points. If that part is not addressed, you lose your opportunity to add those points.*

2. ***You must support each point with facts & examples.*** These demonstrate your clear understanding of the details.

3. ***The essay must be an original synthesis of the information.*** Your instructor wants you to demonstrate your competence in understanding the material, not your ability to

parrot back facts from text and notes.

If you hit these three targets in your essay answer, you will get excellent grades consistently because you have learned how to demonstrate a thorough mastery of the essential information in an organized and concise manner.

MULTIPLE CHOICE & MATCHING: Suppose you have a multiple choice and/or matching (MC/M) test to study for. You will first identify the *type* of MC/M questions from past experience with your instructor's tests or from old tests your instructor has placed on file in the school library. They can either be data-based, concept-based, or mixed.

Here is where previewing and all of the work you did organizing the course material for yourself pays off. Because you have a thorough understanding of the concepts covered in the chapters to be tested, you can answer concept and matching questions more easily.

Data questions can be trickier, because you have no idea which data pieces will be asked. But you can come pretty close to predicting if you refer to your course notes. Review the data that support the main concepts. Remember, instructors want to know if you have the same picture in your head as they have in theirs and there are only so many main concepts in a chapter.

DATA STICKS TO CONCEPTS

Also, remember that as you study concepts, the data come along with them and are easy to recall because they make sense to the whole picture you are building in your head. Now data become not merely isolated little bits of trivia, but meaningful support for the concepts you are studying.

TRUE-FALSE: These are also concept-based, and if you are targeting Level II/ Level III depth in your encoding, you will understand the main concepts and the main data that support them. Usually, instructors will not be looking for the one, tiny exception to the rule (There are exceptions to just about anything.) They are looking for general True and False statements.

SHORT-ANSWER & FILL-INS: Such questions require you to recall and write down what you have learned about the main concepts. The difference is that you will have to generate the answers instead of having them listed for you. For this you will need to encode close to the maximum level of depth and be able to teach the material to another person, using the appropriate terminology. The relationship between the concept and the supporting data will be your target and you will do well if you have focused on encoding both concept and data as a unit. Because you have practiced them with a friend, you will have already

YOU DON'T BECOME A CHAMPION WITHOUT PRACTICE

created the answers from your genuine understanding at least once before.

APPLICATIONS FOR DIFFERENT COURSES

Okay, let's take a look at precise course strategies. Obviously, you can't apply your strategies the same way for every course, and a wise player always adjusts the game plan depending on the opponent. There are differences in the courses that require adjustment, just as various strategies are used against different chess rivals or as coaches scout their opponents to determine a game plan that will win.

As I mentioned before, there are basically 3 types of courses that we will encounter in school: content courses, skill courses, and process courses. To review, an example of a **content** course would be Psychology or History. A content course has a lot of material to read, understand and assimilate into ideas and principles. Courses of this nature require an understanding of course content, because their goal is integration and evaluation of information.

> **THE STRATEGY WILL BE DETERMINED BY THE DIFFERENT COURSE GOALS**

Joan, 18 and an entering freshman, is browsing through the campus bookstore and comes upon the Psychology 101 text she has to buy. As she picks up the seven-pound book she begins to worry, and as she pages through the 789 pages she wonders how she got roped into taking this course. "I'll never be able to read all of this," she mutters to herself. "And if this is only one course, what am I going to do?"

To handle all of this information, Joan will need to

understand the <u>principles</u> behind each chapter and fill in the <u>details</u> as she reads. She will need to put the material into her own words, draw pictures, make charts, differentiate one idea from another, and be able to teach the material to someone else. The more she interacts and works with the material, the better she will do on her tests.

She will also need to determine the type of testing that her instructor requires, because the instructor <u>interprets</u> and <u>directs</u> the course, and every instructor has slightly different goals for his/her students. This will give her the proper viewpoint from which to gather and organize the information as she studies.

This is different from a skill course.

A *skill* course would be a subject like Composition, Languages, or Computer Skills. Such classes require a level of competence based on understanding and practice. Your strategy for skill courses depends in part upon what type of skills learner you are.

Charles and Ray are two different types of skill learners. Charles, 25, is one of those people who reads the entire manual before beginning to use a new tool. He must understand the "model" of how to do something before he feels comfortable. On his recent trip to Europe, Charles would not travel to any country that did not speak a language he had studied in school. For him, understanding the basis of course material is necessary for him to learn comfortably.

On the other hand, Ray, 21, loves to just dive in and figure it out as he goes along. On his trip to Europe he purposely entered countries where he had never experienced the language just to pick up new ways of

> *communicating. He likes to jump into a new task and learn by experience.*

Obviously, these two students will relate differently to a skill course, depending upon the teaching orientation of the instructor. If you are like Charles, you will want to find an instructor who presents theory and structure first, if possible. If you are like Ray, you will look for experiential instruction. In either case, you will want to allow plenty of time for practice in your study calendar. Skills take time and practice to master. Also, if you must take a skills course from an instructor with an opposite communication style, you must

YOU MAY NEED HELP *TRANSLATING* INTO YOUR OWN LEARNING STYLE

allow time for adjusting the instruction to your own way of relating to the course material. This may involve seeking out tutorial help from someone who can help you *translate* into your own style of learning.

Regardless of communication style, these classes require hours of repetitive practice to become fluent in that particular skill. Language study will focus around a clear encoding of grammatical rules and require vocabulary-building tasks involving visiting a language lab or making flash cards.

Process courses involve mental analysis, like Math, Philosophy, Logic or English Literature, where the emphasis is on our ability to reason and evaluate. Because they combine new information with new ways of thinking, they demand consistent attention during class time to get the most from instructor feedback and interaction, as process skills are fine-tuned.

Math is particularly bothersome to many students at this level. More than any other course, math demands practice,

PRACTICE THE PROCESS OF MATHEMATICAL THINKING

practice, practice. Homework is essential and understanding only comes from practicing the process of thinking through problems. You can't get around doing all of your homework, practicing until you can do the problems *cold*.

In process courses, more than any other type, perfect attendance is critical. Here, too, a tutor may make the difference between success and failure, as you have someone help you clarify the principles, practice the process involved and listen as you explain it. A tutor's greatest value is to listen to you explain the process you are following and provide feedback.

Kate, 42, is taking Calculus for the first time and she is having a rough go of it. Not only has it been 24 years since she has been in school, but she hasn't seen a math text since she left. Her best bet is to schedule the course at a time in the day when she is most alert, and allow one or two hours immediately after class to go over what she has just learned and do her homework as soon as humanly possible. She will need to complete all of her homework assignments daily and plan to spend at least one hour a week with either her instructor, a tutor, or another study buddy to work through the material and practice the process.

Notice that I have included literature classes in this category. This is because literature analysis involves critical thinking skills and comparison to past reading. It can only be enriched by social interaction, is based on abstract thought, and requires the same intense concentration during class time.

Testing is usually done by essay. If you are going to communicate your competence successfully at test time, you must follow the thought-model that your instructor uses to approach the material as you are guided through the analytical process. And this is only found in class.

> **FOLLOW YOUR INSTRUCTOR'S THOUGHT MODEL**

Because we are concentrating upon strategy and method for organizing course material, we are predicting and controlling our study efforts. Each of these course types can now be approached with an attitude of complete mastery, because to understand the requirements gives us the competitive edge we need to succeed. In the challenge to master the A's, we have a strategy to win.

SECTION IV
CONCEPTUAL THINKING

Thinking in concepts rather than in incremental details is one of the four major challenges of college level work and is a distinct skill to master. If we can think conceptually, we will find the study process increasingly easier as we practice immediate encoding with the goal of building a complete mental picture. To understand how to do this, it helps to have a mental model of how the brain processes information systematically through to the deepest level of memory (what I call Level III).

The best model I have found is a house (Figure 7) with a single entrance, stairs, and second floor living quarters. The different parts of the house correspond to the principles of encoding necessary for each of the three levels of depth required for different types of test questions.

A HOUSE WITH STAIRS IS THE BEST MENTAL MODEL

Level One of memory is the entry way, Level Two is the stairs to the living areas, and Level Three is the rooms where we can freely live and function. You have access to each level through a door with a key, which is a requirement for entry. You must pass through the areas in order, and there are limits on each area that correspond to different academic goals. *Moving in* to each level requires different operations on the material to be learned. Also, at each level, information is entered (*encoded*), is stored, and may be accessed (*retrieved*) for different tasks, including tests.

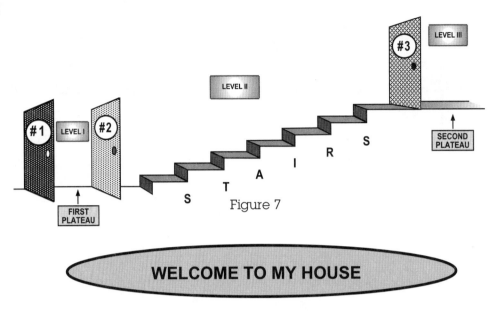

Figure 7

WELCOME TO MY HOUSE

The three parts of my house are the doors, the plateaus, and the stairs.

ENTER THROUGH THE DOORS

THE DOORS. Incoming information must pass through what I call *doors*, with *keys* representing the different requirements to enter the next level. Each of the three doorways provides access to a successively deeper and longer lasting memory experience. You must go through the doors one at a time. You can't jump ahead or expect to reach the deepest level of memory without passing through them in order.

REST ON THE PLATEAUS

THE PLATEAUS. There are two plateaus or resting-places. Each one has a distinct function. The first plateau is often referred to as our *short-term memory*. Items settling here can only be retrieved for a brief period until other items come in to replace them. There is only so much room. However, it is necessary for all new information to cross this threshold. That is the way to the upstairs.

The other plateau, found at the top of the stairs, is the deepest level of understanding and is where information is stored, to be retrieved whenever it is needed in everyday life.

<table>
<tr><td>

CLIMB
THE STAIRS

</td><td>

THE STAIRS. Level Two consists of a staircase of seven stairs, because understanding keeps increasing steadily as it is grouped together and elaborated.

</td></tr>
</table>

Understanding increases; it never stands still. You can't live and function in Level Two any more than you can live on the stairs of your home. In fact, one step propels you to the next almost automatically, fueled by your natural drive to make sense of the world at all costs. That is simply how we all operate as thinking beings.

WALKING THROUGH THE MODEL

Information first comes to the door of *selective attention*, the front door of the entire memory process that makes Level I memory immediately accessible.

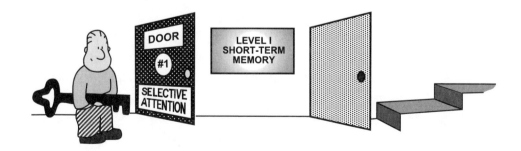

Figure 8

DOOR #1. Welcome to my house. I am going to greet you at the front door and let you in. The doorway

> **OPEN DOOR #1: *SELECTIVE ATTENTION***

is not large enough for more than one person to enter at a time, but several people may stand comfortably in the entrance. This is the way our selective attention operates. We can focus on only one thing at a time, and several *bits* of information may be present in our immediate memory (the entry way) at once. It is like the quip, "What you see is what you get." Whatever you choose to attend to is what gets in the door. What we pay attention to is what gets programmed. This is the key.

The average is between 5 and 9 (7, plus or minus 2) *bits*. No more, no matter how hard we try. Just like my home's entry area, if another *bit* enters, one is pushed out (like my friends on a busy party night). Holding things in this area (called our *short-term memory*) is therefore very limited and we can't rely on it for academic tasks, although everything we remember must pass through it. After all, it is still only the front door.

> *Sandra is studying hard for her Biology test. The instructor has given out a list of 50 terms for the chapters they have covered and Sandra is trying to remember them all. As she reads down the list of unfamiliar terms, she stops cold. "I can't get through 10 of these words without forgetting the first ones! What am I going to do?" Sandra has discovered that the normal brain can only handle 5 to 9 pieces of information at once in short-term memory. She has attended to them and they are in the front door, but without <u>doing</u> something with them, that is as far as they will go. She certainly can't rely on her short-term memory for the test.*

> *Sandra needs to think conceptually if she is ever going to do well in Biology.*

All course material must enter this door to be *encoded*. *Encoding* refers to how information is taken into our minds for retention. Such operations as reading notes and textbooks or hearing audio tapes qualify as gathering information for encoding. The greatest mistake we students make is to think that reading the text and notes is what *study* is all about. This is essential, but it is only the first step, much like going to the lumberyard to buy materials to build a

READING THE TEXTBOOK AND NOTES IS NOT STUDY

home. Just gathering materials is not building the house. You cannot live in a pile of lumber, yet we often try. We limit our memory because we do not take the information any further. Study is original organization of the information, and anything less does not qualify.

How many times have we, as students, put ourselves down for "having a bad memory," yet all we have done is let the information in the front door? We never gave our memory a

GIVE YOUR MEMORY A CHANCE TO WORK

chance. Everyone's memory works this way and it is time for us to recognize that what appears to be a personal limitation is merely a product of the brain hardware we are born with.

This is actually quite adaptive. I would not want to remember everything I had ever read, only what was significant and useful. Realizing this, we can move on to tasks that allow the important course material to move into our home and be easy to recall whenever we need to use it.

The way information enters depends on how we attend to it, and to think conceptually, we need to focus on organizing information the first time that we read it. Our goals determine

> **THE <u>WAY</u> WE ATTEND TO INFORMATION IS THE WAY IT ENTERS**

what we encode and our mental focus at any time automatically prioritizes incoming information. We filter our surroundings to fit our priorities and we have control over how information enters our minds by directing our priorities. If our goal is to organize, we lay the groundwork for conceptual thought.

Prioritization is what selective attention is all about. If all possible information pushed through the front door at once, there is no way we could possibly handle it. It would be an uncontrolled mental stampede. So, our brain is smart enough to only let one piece in at a time so we may handle it effectively, and how we direct our brain to organize things determines just what comes in.

> **THE BRAIN PRIORITIZES AUTOMATICALLY**

Here is an example: we have all had the strange experience of reading a paragraph or even a whole chapter, our eyes passing over the little black marks on the pages and then realizing that we do not remember anything about what we have just read. How can that be?

Well, reading and understanding are not necessarily the same thing. It depends upon what we have directed our brain to look for (our goal or the focus we have chosen for ourselves). This focus is encoded along with the words.

I can remember sitting in the library with my eyes blankly passing over little black words simply because I was attending to the goal, "Read pages 345-397," but couldn't

READING & UNDERSTANDING ARE 2 DIFFERENT THINGS

remember what I had read if you offered me straight A's and a million bucks! Wasn't I attending to the text? No. I was attending to, "Read pages 345-397," not the meaning, so this was *all I got.* (Remember, *What you see -- focus on -- is what you get.*) The number of pages was my goal, so the content was virtually ignored, and certainly only understood dimly, at best.

I can also remember times where I had to find the answer to a question and zeroed in on it right away because I was looking for it. In the first instance, I didn't remember the text, and in the second, I never forgot it because my attention was <u>directed</u> differently. Because information is encoded as a unit, we can only remember what we attend to IN THE **WAY** WE ATTEND TO IT.

To think conceptually, then, is to seek to organize all new information into a condensed form. We are seeking an overview, a summary, the basic root of the ideas we are learning. This allows us to build mental pictures that we can modify and refer to as we go along.

What is Sandra going to do? She has a list of 50 terms she must remember, but only 9 of them stick at once. She needs to seek out some form of basic grouping or organization of these terms so that there will be a basis for the next level of thinking and effective recall.

While it is essential for *bits*, or individual details to enter through the doorway of our selective attention, this entry is not a place for information to live and function because it is limited. Who wants to eat, sleep and relax in the small area beside the front door? To enter more deeply into the home where we can carry on normal life, we want to go to the living areas on the second floor. So we move toward the base of the

THERE IS NO MEMORY WITHOUT MEANING

stairs and face Door #2, our pathway to the *living area* above. To get information any deeper into our memory, we need to pass through this second door, using the key of *meaning*.

. To pass into the second level of memory, the information that entered Level I must have meaning (Figure 9). This is not always the case. You may have rote-memorized the words to "La Bamba" but not understand Spanish. Or you may remember an acronym for the first letter of each of the 12 cranial nerves in human anatomy, but what they are or what they do may <u>mean</u> nothing to you. Memory tricks (mnemonics) are useful to a point, but it definitely does not work to build your knowledge base on trivia. In fact, couldn't one definition of trivia be information without significance?

Figure 9

DOOR #2. Since we want to remember what we have attended to, it MUST mean something to us. It may relate to other things we have learned, it may promise to be the answer to an important problem, or it may be this week's assigned course topic, but it must MEAN SOMETHING or it will not be encoded for later retrieval.

If I attend to information looking at what it means, I have access to the stairs. Before me lie seven steps I can climb to process the new information as I develop my concept. At first glance, the final plateau looks very high and far away, but then I notice that, like all sets of stairs, each one is very small and easy to manage. As I go up the steps I am going through what researchers call elaboration of the material I am learning. Without elaboration it is impossible to remember anything for long periods of time, so it is essential that I make this climb.

It looks like a lot of work at first, but a funny thing happens. As I reach one step, I find myself propelled along to the next and it is virtually impossible to stop building my conceptual model of the details. Somehow, just taking that first step is the biggest hurdle to remembering, because that is how I become active in the climb. It is a mental shift from <u>passive</u>

CLIMBING THE STAIRS IS ALMOST AUTOMATIC

to <u>active</u> behavior (another of the challenges of college freshmen), and I must become involved with the course material in order to succeed. I must get my mental feet moving, my brain organizing and analyzing details, and once active, I keep going. My mind behaves like a walking spring toy, automatically seeking the next step.

An additional bonus is that taking control of information like this actually creates enjoyment in a subject. Any subject. In fact, whatever subject we understand thoroughly becomes one that we like.

> *Sandra takes another look at her list of 50 Biology terms. As she looks at them as ideas with meaning, able to be organized, and not just words on a page, she begins to ascend the 7 Steps of Elaboration. She is actually exhilarated by the feeling that she is thinking independently as she creates her own grouping of the words and organization of the details.*

While the entrance can be visualized as Level I of our memory, the stairs can be visualized as Level II (Figure 10).

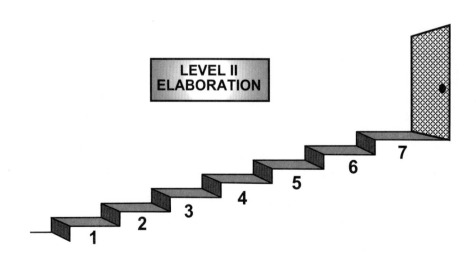

Figure 10

CLIMBING THE 7 STEPS OF ELABORATION

The first step is that we understand the material.

STEP 1: UNDERSTANDING

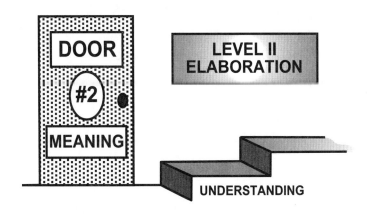

Figure 11

This does not imply that we have to know everything about the topic all at once. We must simply understand the individual ideas as they are presented. This takes information past the rudimentary level of recognizing key words and into the realm of study.

> *First, Sandra went over the 50 Biology terms to understand the basic definitions. What is this term talking about? What is this one actually referring to?*
> *She went past the glossary definitions and started to understand the ideas she was working with.*

Next, we look for similarities between data pieces.

STEP 2: GROUP SIMILAR IDEAS TOGETHER

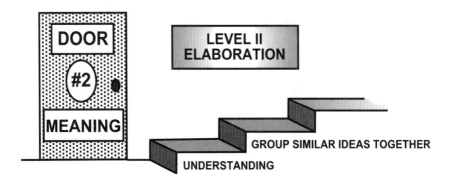

Figure 12

As we look at information we have read or heard, we notice similar terms or ideas that seem related to each other. These we group together.

Next, Sandra organized similar or related Biology terms together into groups.

STEP 3: SEE THE RELATIONSHIPS BETWEEN GROUPS OF IDEAS

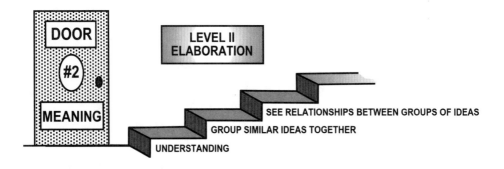

Figure 13

As you have noticed, it is very difficult to group and not see the relationships between them. Obviously, you are using some category system to group the terms. But there is a tiny difference. In observing the relationships between groups of ideas, you find the crude beginning of the *critical thinking* process, which forms the basis for advanced analysis and most tests.

Then, Sandra noticed how the categories under which she grouped the terms fit together.

STEP 4: IDENTIFY AND LABEL THE PRINCIPLES

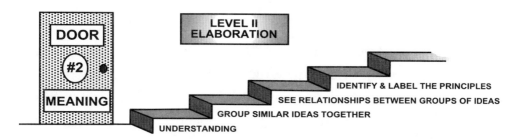

Figure 14

It is almost impossible to group, compare and contrast information without consciously identifying the principles involved, but actually <u>labeling</u> these principles *sets them in stone.* Even if you forget the details, the principles are there for future reference and the details are easy to fit in later, the next time you review.

Sandra made a chart of all of the categories she noticed and listed terms that fell under each one beneath the titles.

> **NOTE:** The <u>sole</u> purpose for review before a test to remind us of details. If you find that you are trying to grasp concepts at the last minute, that is a warning sign that you are not organizing <u>early</u> enough in the process.

STEP 5: PUT THE INFORMATION INTO YOUR OWN WORDS

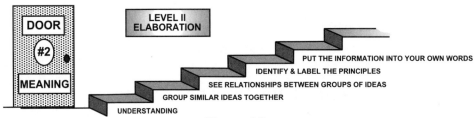

Figure 15

Now we get to the fun part. We get to create our own ideas about the course material and venture into independent

> **ORIGINAL IDEAS ARE REWARDING**

thought, which is the third challenge of college-level thinking. Actually, all of this is so easy and challenging that it is what our minds call fun. Yes, I'm serious! If this is not true, then why are board games like

checkers and chess so popular, if not for the challenge to control a situation with fixed rules, small, achievable goals and the mental reward of winning because of our brilliant, original thought? When we have control of our efforts, we really like to study.

Research has shown repeatedly that when students relate the material in the text to themselves in some way, they hardly ever forget it. This can be done by applying the ideas to daily life or by remembering examples from past experience, but the easiest and most practical technique to apply is to simply put it

<u>into your own words</u>. This is the automatic result of identifying the differences and relationships between information pieces.

> *Sandra took her chart and added distinguishing details beside the terms as well as notes of her own that helped her remember the differences. As a result, she ended up with a clear breakdown of the chapter material.*

> *Roy could relate to his assignment in American History because he remembered reading some of it before. Not only that, but he had debated one of the topics for speech class and had to put it into his own words. As he grouped more of the facts, dates and names together, he began to form a mental concept of what took place during those years. It became meaningful to him and he could discuss it freely. As a result, he found that the information was much easier to understand and remember when he was asked questions in class and he even contributed his own thoughts to the class session. His teacher seemed impressed by his questions, even though Roy did not know all of the answers.*

From here, it is hard to restrain yourself from Step 6.

STEP 6: VERBALIZE THE INFORMATION

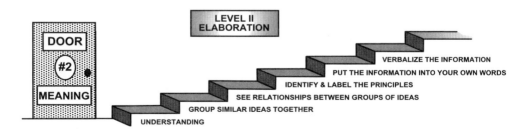

Figure 16

> *Jack nearly leaped out of his chair when he realized how the periodic table of the elements works. He let out a whoop of joy and ran into the kitchen to tell his roommate what he had discovered for himself.*

Jack didn't have to be told Step 6. In fact, if his friend hadn't been there, he would have told the doorknob. When we understand something for ourselves, just try and stop us from telling someone else. *Aha* experiences like this are exhilarating, and excitement is part of that momentous discovery.

STORE THE INFORMATION IN MORE THAN ONE AREA OF THE BRAIN

There is method to this madness of oral presentation. The greater the number of different ways we relate to the material at hand, the greater the number of brain cells (neurons) that become involved with the information in different areas of the cerebral cortex. Reading involves only a few areas of the brain, while reading, sorting, organizing, hearing and speaking involve areas responsible for language, thought, hearing, memories of past experiences and spatial relationships. The process of translating information from reading to speech is quite complex and rich with neural interconnections that all get involved with the material.

> *Sandra felt silly, but she found herself explaining her term groupings to her cat, Dimples. It felt good to explain her new discovery of how all of these details fit together, and just talking about it set the information further into her memory.*

To put the final cap on your understanding, move up to Step 7.

STEP 7: TEACH IT TO SOMEONE ELSE

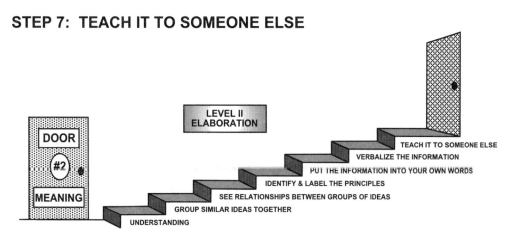

Figure 17

Cats are fine, but humans are even better because they ask questions and can tell you when you may not make sense. They can also ask questions about information that will send you back to your books looking for further answers. That is just what you want. The more you can refine your concepts, the longer you will remember them, and the more prepared you are for your exams.

> *Sandra found her classmate Laura studying in the women's lounge. She explained all of her Biology terms and the relationships between them to her in less than an hour. Laura asked some good questions which helped Sandra realize some areas that were still not clear to her.*
>
> *After the girls finished, they both had a better understanding of the entire chapter. Because she had started the study process early in the week, Sandra had an opportunity to review her personal organization daily until*

> the test. Even two years later, when Sandra took Anatomy, she remembered most of the terms with only a brief review.

WELCOME TO THE TOP

Well, here we are at the top of the stairs. We have built a conceptual, mental picture of our course material. That wasn't so hard, was it? Not really, and it was actually fun, once we knew just what to DO with the information we had to learn.

Before us lies the third and last door, the gateway to a fully useful base of information. It leads into the living areas of our home, where we can function freely and draw from all of our past memories comfortably, whenever we need them to solve a new problem. This is Level III, the level of practical use. It is here that we want to place our new concepts neatly on a shelf in our mind, so that

LET'S MOVE IN

whenever we want them we can access them easily.

This deepest level of memory processing is the storehouse for all of the concepts, memories and experiences that we refer to and use each day. This final door and its key are attachment to personal experience and by teaching the information to someone else, the final step of Level II, we have reached that threshold quite easily. Information that is useful is information that is never forgotten, and personally used information loses its strangeness and becomes a natural part of the way we think and act.

Figure 18

DOOR #3. Why is this necessary? Isn't it enough to attend to information, understand it and elaborate it over the seven steps? Well, research has shown repeatedly that whatever you actively use, you never lose. Also, anything that can be encoded originally is remembered longer and in a more useful form than

**OPEN
DOOR #3:
*ATTACHMENT
TO PERSONAL
EXPERIENCE***

information that is not. For this reason, whatever you want to remember for long periods of time and need to be able to use MUST be organized personally and originally.

Sandra found this out when she made sure she understood the 50 Biology terms she was studying and followed the 7 steps to elaborate the material they represented. Then, when she related them to her own personal experience and practiced using them, she remembered 100% of the material and aced her exam. Not only that, but she now saw Biology as challenging, but easy, because the task was clearly defined and she was in control of a manageable process.

This is the final goal of study, to be able to have the information catalogued into categories, stored within easy reach whenever we are tested on it. We can also reach it whenever we need to refer to it in conversation, to use it at home relating to others, to research further information on the topic, to understand more advanced material, or simply to play trivia games.

Whenever we practice using the material in some way, our memory for it is strengthened, It is comfortable for us to have our closets full of organized information. Gathering it and bringing it up the stairs, to be stored where we may actively use it, is the process of education. When our cupboards are full, we are the most content, because then we are prepared for whatever kind of test the instructor may give us on any information, not to mention the other uses it will have for us.

**EDUCATION =
CONTENT
+
PROCESS**

91

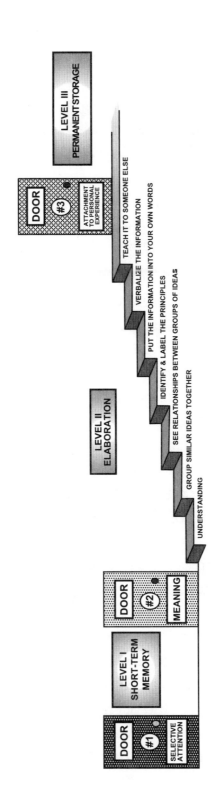

Figure 19

SECTION V
PAY ATTENTION TO DETAILS

No book on the topic of academic success is complete without a chapter on the importance of details. There are 4 types of details a student must watch out for:

1. Details in course requirements.
2. Details in assignment requirements.
3. Details in note taking.
4. Details in written presentation.

First of all NEVER ASSUME ANYTHING. This can kill your grade faster than any other single mental mistake. You cannot assume that every math class has the same homework / exam point balance or that every psychology teacher uses the same grading scale. You cannot assume that all assignments are graded according to the same standards. You cannot assume that whenever you miss class that nothing happened when you were gone. You cannot assume that presenting written material without correcting all grammatical errors or not following a recognized presentation style for your term paper will give you top grades just because of your brilliant ideas.

1. Details in course requirements.

You must read the course syllabus and use it regularly to chart your progress. This document is a contract between you and the instructor that lists the grading requirements, course expectations, and other pertinent information. In other words, it tells you the rules of the game.

You would never even play a casual game with your friends without knowing the rules, let alone a *game* with such high stakes as your academic transcript, yet some students fail courses simply because they assume that academic requirements are always the same. Students every term stash

<table>
<tr><td>THE SYLLABUS TELLS YOU THE RULES</td></tr>
</table>

their syllabi in the back of their notebook and never look at them after the first day of class. (Every term, I have to give additional ones to students who have lost them.)

What happens when you are absent? Your syllabus addresses attendance, so you will know whether and how you can make up the points missed, or if attendance is even counted towards the grade. Teachers and classes differ.

When are the assignments due? If you know, you can pace yourself and not be caught stressfully completing several at the last minute for different classes.

How are grades compiled? Are they based only on exams? How much does a term paper count? What about class participation? Are there pop quizzes? Are tests given on the same day of the week? Monday, Friday, or otherwise? All of these will affect your term strategy and rhythm and they are all found in the syllabus. This is the single most important set of papers in your notebook and should be guarded carefully.

2.   **Details in assignment requirements.**

Every assignment has a purpose. It is trying to develop a distinct aspect of your educational package. It is molding your mental repertoire into a more complete product. Since they are all as different as the courses you take, you can never assume that what is required for one is required for all of the others. For example, I try to teach my students the APA (American Psychological Association) style for writing papers. I grade heavily on details, one point off for each type of mistake. Yet, despite 2 hours of class time and several detailed handouts with examples and a complete scoring breakdown, a few students every term hand in papers that never refer to the model provided. They never read the handouts and never took notes. They ASSUME that they know how to write a

> **EACH ASSIGNMENT HAS A DIFFERENT PURPOSE**

paper and that is good enough. (By the way, these are usually the same ones who lose their syllabi, so it seems to be a pattern of not attending to detail.)

Ask your teacher about the purpose and format of the assignment and the standard of grading to be used. This is good academic communication.

3.   Details in note taking.

If you miss a class, for heaven's sake, GET THE NOTES. It is actually an insult to your instructors to assume that the lectures they prepare, the time, effort and expense they spend traveling to school, and the effort they expend presenting the information to the class are not important and contribute nothing to your understanding of the material. Also, you may have missed significant logistical information like syllabus revisions, study sheets, handouts, and class cancellation dates.

> **LECTURES GIVE STRUCTURE TO THE COURSE**

Note taking is critical because this is how you find out what your instructor considers important about the material. Lectures give structure to the course. If you can learn to think like your instructor, you will have help encoding course information in the same way it will be tested. Never go into a test without complete class notes.

At the beginning of the term, swap phone numbers with at least two people that you can use as backup for your notes. That way, you will save valuable time searching for them.

4. Details in written presentation.

This is more critical than either students or even many instructors realize. I did my masters' thesis on how misspelling as few as 5.9% of the words in a written assignment will affect not only the grade given, but also how the instructor perceives the non-academic character of the student. Even though the instructors were directed to consider only argumentation and thought quality, students were graded down an average of half a grade simply due to misspellings. Students' personal

WRITTEN WORK IS A REPRESENTATION OF YOUR COMPETENCE

characters were also evaluated lower on 10 different dimensions (including honesty and punctuality) simply because of a few spelling errors.

Just like a finish carpenter may enhance or devalue a well-built home by the quality of his work, so writing mechanics can either make or break a well-thought-out written project. The successful student must pay exquisite detail to writing style (MLA or APA), spelling, grammar, punctuation, margins, spacing, paper quality, print tone and even font type to present written work worthy of top grades. You cannot go into an important job interview with a glob of mustard on your shirt and leave the impression that you are a neat and careful person, even though is was your daughter who soiled you on the way over in the car. First impressions count and excuses are not acceptable.

There is an important rule of thumb: <u>anything</u> that interferes with communication between student and instructor, that makes it harder to grade a paper, will lower that grade significantly. One study showed that even excessively advanced vocabulary decreased, rather than increased, grades. (Not writing clearly hinders communication because it is a bother to stop and decipher it.) This principle applies to unclear handwriting, poor grammar or punctuation, not following style instructions, or even a coffee stain on the paper.

BE CLEAR
****
BE CORRECT
****
FOLLOW INSTRUCTIONS

I have compiled a checklist below that outlines the standard technical requirements for college level work. Be sure to check with each teacher to make sure that all grading targets for that assignment are covered in this list so that your bases are covered. Never assume anything.

REQUIREMENTS FOR COLLEGE QUALITY WORK

1. **Word processed or typed.**
   [Note: If you have a choice, word processed yields better grades.]

2. **Double spaced.**

3. **Type is dark enough to read easily.**

4. **#12 or #14 font (like this size--some font styles have a very small #12).**

5. **Plain, book-style font, NO SCRIPT.**

6. **1" margins on all 4 sides of the paper.**

7. DO NOT justify the right margin.

8. Indent the first line in a paragraph 5 spaces from the left margin. NO BLOCK STYLE (that is a business format).

9. No spelling errors (use a computer spelling check AND have it proofed by at least one other person).

10. No grammatical errors (proofed by at least one other person).

11. No punctuation errors (proofed by at least one other person).

12. Research papers may require either APA* or MLA** format for the title page, footnotes (or in-text citations), reference page, quotations and other details. These are distinctly different. Check with your instructor to verify which style is expected and identify the specific requirements for your assignment.

* American Psychological Association
** Modern Language Association

SECTION VI
ELIMINATE STRESS

Any good coach knows that in order to perform its best, a team must play loose, free from anxiety. It is also well known that stress actually *short-circuits* our memory retrieval system,

STRESS SHORT-CIRCUITS MEMORY RETRIEVAL

making complete recall of information almost impossible. Stress at test time is definitely something we do not need.

Because we get stressed by entering into new situations with no mental management plan, we can use the strategies we have discussed to virtually eliminate test anxiety.

Since research has shown that the four basics of stress are mind set, unpredictability, uncontrollability and social support, let's make a checklist of stress-reducers and see how we have taken care of them through the rules we have discussed. We know that to eliminate the stress involved in study, we must be able to:

✔ **KEEP AN ATTITUDE OF COMPLETE SUCCESS**

Procrastination kills memory. I can do this. I will do it now. I am prepared. I understand this completely. We looked at how dramatically attitude works on our grades and saw that students who take control of their course work, don't procrastinate and have the attitude of *whatever it takes*, feel like they have control, are free from anxiety and therefore are successful in their courses. You have heard it before, but I'll say it once again:

ATTITUDE IS EVERYTHING!

Don't get intimidated by a particular course just because you have heard it is *hard*. *Hard* simply means that you don't have a clear picture of the material and *easy* means that you do. It rarely has to do with the material itself, simply how clearly it is presented and what you do with the information before test time. I often have heard two students in the same class declare it to be both *hard* and *easy*, with their grades reflecting their opinions.

> *HARD* = "I DON'T HAVE A CLEAR PICTURE"

> *EASY* = "I HAVE A CLEAR PICTURE"

All *hard* means is that:

1.   the person who told you it was hard never did master it, OR

2.   it is a challenge to encode the material <u>because one of the keys to the 3 doors is MISSING</u>:

Key to Door I -- Attention: it is a challenge to attend to the information (boring lecturer, poorly written text, distractions in the study environment)

Key to Door II -- Meaning: course information may take longer to clarify (much information, vague concepts, lecture different than text)

Key to Door III -- Relation to Personal Experience: lack of prior experience with that topic (not taking prerequisites, not elaborating information or not taking it to the level of being able to teach it to someone else).

If you can get past all of the mental obstacles and look at the information as a challenge, rather than a threat, you will be in for a fascinating game of you vs. the course. More often than not, once you have cracked the code and succeeded, the overwhelming sense of accomplishment will encourage you to tackle even *harder* courses, because you can do it, where others have failed.

> **NOTHING FEELS BETTER THAN TO HAVE ACED A *HARD* CLASS**

✔ **PREDICT COURSE TASKS**

We've done that by organizing our study time for the entire term and logging all of our due dates and time available for study onto our wall calendar. We can predict, all right. Being able to predict what is coming removes the greatest source of anxiety. Lab rats that were subject to conditions

> **PREDICTION EMPOWERS**

they couldn't predict became ill, and it is no surprise. Just look how you feel when your instructor announces a pop quiz! The simple act of knowing what to expect gives us a sense of control, and from there we can break down course expectations into smaller tasks that will lead us to complete success.

Also, we have consistently followed the 16 rules for effective study and climbed the 7 steps of elaboration. By doing this, we have been able to:

✔ **ESTABLISH CONTROL**

Boy, that feels good! Now I can take on the world. The Dean's List is no obstacle now.

The more we can do to establish a sense of control, the

better our memory recall will be. When we eliminate stress we open the doors for recall. It does no good to encode information if we cannot recall it when we need to use it.

Using that *master calendar* really helps. Every day when

> **CONTROL =
> LESS ANXIETY =
> BETTER MEMORY**

I walk by my desk, I can see what I have coming up in the weeks ahead. All of my activities fall into place and take on a regular rhythm. If I have an event to attend, I can get my

assignments done <u>before</u> I leave, so I'm not stressed when I get back. I can pace my study time for exams to allow at least the minimum 2 days necessary for my mind to process new material. With this sense of predictability and total control, my classes are manageable, although they are still a lot of work.

Because I have been keeping contact with my instructor and have been asking all of my questions, clarifying what I can't understand on my own, and since I have been explaining my course material to my friend, I have fulfilled the fourth requirement for eliminating stress:

✔ **ESTABLISH SOCIAL SUPPORTS**

Education is a social process because it involves transfer of ideas from one mind to another. We do not learn in a vacuum and we do not test out in a vacuum, either. Someone

> **EDUCATION
> IS A
> SOCIAL
> PROCESS**

assigns the material and someone makes up the tests, so communication with that someone (your instructor) is most important. You may also find that getting a tutor who can discuss concepts with you one-on-one is a tremendous help in clarifying ideas.

And, as you have noticed, teaching the material to a partner helps tremendously as we try to assimilate it all.

We cannot minimize the importance of others in the study process or we will lose. Don't try to do it alone. Ask questions and discuss answers. Mutual support benefits everyone.

SECTION VII
SUMMARY & CONCLUSION

Memory research teaches us a lot about how to study in college. To review, we have learned that study is organization, that we need to take active control of the process, that we must attend to information carefully, time our study efforts properly, organize and elaborate material into concepts, and explain the material to someone else to set it into our minds for long-term retention.

The orderly principles I have laid out work. In fact, the research for this book began from student input. One term a few years ago in Introductory Psychology, I had a struggling student go from F's and D's to A's in one week. The difference was night and day. I called him aside and asked him what he had changed to create such a drastic difference in his grades. He answered, "We just went over the chapter on memory. I saw what I was doing wrong."

In subsequent semesters, I informally polled my students to find out which chapters they felt had contributed most to their education. Without fail, the memory chapter was at the top of the list. After that, I began to research human memory for the answers to the questions I saw students facing every day and which I had faced as an incoming freshman years ago. Now, every term, students tell me of dramatic improvements when they employ these study techniques in their courses.

This understanding of human memory and how it can be applied has helped students with difficult work schedules and family responsibilities make it through school. It has given hope to students struggling with learning disabilities. It has provided direction to athletes dealing with road trips and demanding practice schedules. It has guided students returning to school after many years' absence to develop a successful, personal study system. It has increased confidence, shortened study hours and raised grades for many others.

Academics is serious business. Often our future earning power, status, and ultimate net worth hang upon the results of this all-powerful mental contest. Also, self-confidence is tied to our perception of competence and academic failure can doom us to assess ourselves unfairly and discourage us from success before we even step up to the plate to try. In the arena of life, these are high stakes, and not to be taken lightly. Therefore, the little book you have just read may be the single most important piece of information you will ever read because it takes away all excuses and lays out a solid plan for academic success.

Over all, there is nothing like the exhilarating feeling of a game well played, when the clock runs out and the score is in your favor. In education, all *games* are championship games, the scores are written in transcript-quality stone and your merit as a person to be reckoned with is judged by these indelible memoirs of your expertise. It is my sincere wish that all of your *hard* courses may become *easy* ones, that you may experience unprecedented success, and that you find education to be an exciting and abundantly rewarding enterprise. May all of your grades be aces and may you always use good Study Sense.

APPENDIX I
SUMMARY OF MEMORY LEVELS, ENTRY KEYS & TESTING REQUIREMENTS

	ENCODING	STORAGE	RETRIEVAL
LEVEL I:	Read Text & Notes	Superficial	Superficial Cues

ENTRY: *Selective Attention*
MAXIMUM TESTING LEVEL: *Recognition (Key-Word Multiple Choice)*

	ENCODING	STORAGE	RETRIEVAL
LEVEL II:	Understanding & Elaboration	Comprehensive	Comprehensive Cues

ENTRY: *Meaning*
MAXIMUM TESTING LEVEL: *Comprehension (Concept-Based Multiple Choice, Matching, True-False, Fill-in, Short Answer)*

	ENCODING	STORAGE	RETRIEVAL
LEVEL III:	Personal Organization	Integrated With Life Expereinces	Active Use Cues

ENTRY: *Attachment to Personal Experience*
MAXIMUM TESTING LEVEL: *Application (Essay)*

APPENDIX II
REASONS WHY PROCRASTINATION *KILLS* MEMORY

1. **LACK OF CONTROL CREATES ANXIETY**
    &
    ANXIETY SHORT-CIRCUITS MEMORY
    LOSS OF CONTROL = HELPLESSNESS
    HELPLESSNESS = ANXIETY
    ANXIETY = SHORT-CIRCUITED MEMORY

2. **MEMORIES ARE SET BY GOING OVER NEW INFORMATION A SECOND TIME <u>IMMEDIATELY</u>**

3. **IT TAKES <u>AT LEAST 2 DAYS</u> FOR THE BRAIN TO PROCESS NEW INFORMATION COMPLETELY**

4. **MEMORIES ARE PROCESSED INTO LONG-TERM STORAGE DURING REM (DREAM) SLEEP. NO SLEEP BECAUSE OF CRAMMING AND / OR ALL NIGHTERS TOTALLY DEFEATS THE PURPOSE**

APPENDIX III
SUMMARY OF THE 16 RULES FOR EFFECTIVE STUDY

ORGANIZATION AND MORE ORGANIZATION

RULE #1   GET RID OF DISTRACTIONS

RULE #2   ALWAYS READ WITH PENCIL & PAPER, TAKING NOTES

RULE #3   CREATE CLEAR BREAKS BETWEEN SUBJECTS

RULE #4   NOTICE THE DIFFERENCES BETWEEN TERMS & IDEAS

RULE #5   GROUP BOOK & LECTURE NOTES TOGETHER BY TOPIC

RULE #6   MAKE YOUR OWN COMPARE & CONTRAST CHARTS

RULE #7   LOOK UP INFORMATION YOU ARE NOT SURE ABOUT

RULE #8   DRAW & COLOR CODE PICTURES, CHARTS & DIAGRAMS

RULE #9   STUDY FOR THE TYPE OF TEST YOU WILL TAKE

IT'S ALL IN THE TIMING

RULE #10   READ & REVIEW IMMEDIATELY AFTER CLASS

RULE #11   STUDY ONE SECTION AT A TIME & KEEP IT SHORT

RULE #12   REVIEW YOUR TEXT & LECTURE NOTES DAILY

RULE #13   GET A GOOD NIGHT'S SLEEP AFTER STUDY

OVERLEARNING ENSURES RETENTION

RULE #14   RELATE THE INFORMATION TO YOUR LIFE

RULE #15   EXPLAIN THE INFORMATION TO SOMEONE ELSE

RULE #16   MAKE UP A PRACTICE TEST & SWAP WITH A BUDDY

APPENDIX IV
REQUIREMENTS FOR COLLEGE QUALITY WORK

1. Word processed or typed. [Note: If you have a choice, word processed yields better grades.]

2. Double spaced.

3. Type is dark enough to read easily.

4. #12 or #14 font (like this size--some font styles have a very small #12).

5. Plain, book-style font, NO SCRIPT.

6. 1" margins on all 4 sides of the paper.

7. DO NOT justify the right margin.

8. Indent the first line in a paragraph 5 spaces from the left margin. NO BLOCK STYLE (that is a business format).

9. No spelling errors (use a computer spelling check AND have it proofed by at least one other person).

10. No grammatical errors (proofed by at least one other person).

11. No punctuation errors (proofed by at least one other person).

12. Research papers may require either APA* or MLA** format for the title page, footnotes (or in-text citations), reference page, quotations and other details. These are distinctly different. Check with your instructor to verify which style is expected and identify the specific requirements for your assignment.

*   American Psychological Association
** Modern Language Association

APPENDIX V
USING GOOD STUDY SENSE
A PRACTICAL, STEP-BY STEP SUMMARY

1. Make a master calendar.
    ❖ include all course topics, assignments, tests, fun activities, free time

2. Allow at least 2 days to process new information.
    ❖ let your brain "chew" the material; processing information takes time

3. Preview all of your text chapters for the week.
    ❖ this is much faster & easier than reading it completely the first time through [& it has the same effect]

4. Organize the information while reading it the first time.
    ❖ create your own picture of the material as you take book notes

5. Organize for distinctiveness.
    ❖ make clear distinctions between concepts, events, key words, etc.

6. Organize for short periods of time.
    ❖ never encode for more than 1 hour at a time [20 min. is best]; no TV between sessions

7. "Layer" information with space in between.
    ❖ review all book & text notes every day for 15 minutes

8. Get all of your questions answered before the test.
    ❖ go into the test with a clear picture of the information

9. Explain key terms / concepts to someone else.
    ❖ if you can explain it, it is "yours" and you will never forget it

10. Rehearse taking the test.
    ❖ create a practice test and swap with someone else

References

Anderson, R.C., & Pichert, J.W. (1978). Recall of previously unrecallable information following a shift in perspective. Journal of Verbal Learning and Verbal Behavior, 17 (1), 1-12.

Ashcraft, M.H., Kellas, G, & Needham, S. (1975). Rehearsal and retrieval processes in free recall of categorized lists. Memory and Cognition, 3 (5), 506-512.

Baddeley, A.D. (1986). Working memory. Oxford: Oxford University Press II.

Barsalou, L.W. (1993). Flexibility, structure, and linguistic vagary in concepts: Manifestations of a compositional system of perceptual symbols. In Collins, A.F., Gathercole, S.E., Conway, M.A., Morris, P.E., (Eds.) Theories of memory. Hove, United Kingdom: Lawrence Erlbaum Associates.

Bartlett, J.C. (1977). Effects of immediate testing on delayed retrieval: Search and recovery operations with four types of cue. Journal of Experimental Psychology: Human Learning and Memory, 3 (6), 719-732.

Begg, I. (1978). Similarity and contrast in memory for relations. Memory and Cognition, 6 (5), 509-517.

Bjork, R.A., & Whitten, W.B. (1974). Recency-sensitive retrieval processes in long-term free recall. Cognitive Psychology, 6 (2), 173-189.

Bransford, J.D. & Johnson, M.K. (1972). Contextual prerequisites for understanding: Some investigations of comprehension and recall. Journal of Verbal Learning and Verbal behavior, 11 (6), 717-726.

Cohen, G., Kiss, G., & LeVoi, M. (1993). Memory: Current issues. Buckingham, United Kingdom: Open University Press.

Craik, F.I.M., & Lockhart, R.S. (1972). Levels of processing: A framework for memory research. Journal of Verbal Learning and Verbal Behavior, 11 (6), 671-684.

Craik, F.I.M., & Tulving, E. (1975). Depth of processing and the relation of words in episodic memory. Journal of Experimental Psychology: General, 104 (3), 268-294.

Crovitz, H.F., & Harvey, M.T. (1979). Visual imagery vs. semantic category as encoding conditions. Bulletin of the Psychonomic Society, 13 (5), 291-292.

Dickinson, D.J., & O'Connell, D.Q. (1990). Effect of quality and quantity of study on student grades. Journal of Educational Research, 83, (4), 227-231.

Driskell, J.E., Willis, R.P., & Copper, C. (1992). Effect of overlearning on retention. Journal of Applied Psychology, 77 (5), 615-622.

Dunn, J.C., & Kirsner, K. (1989). Implicit memory: Task or process? In Implicit memory: Theoretical issues. Lewandowsky, S., Dunn, J.C., & Kirsner, K., eds. Hillsdale, NJ: Lawrence Erlbaum Associates.

Einstein, G.O., & Hunt, R.R. (1980). Levels of processing and organization: Addictive effects of individual-item and relational processing. Journal of Experimental Psychology: Human Learning and Memory, 6 (5), 588-598.

Ellis, H.C., & Hunt, R.R. (1993). Fundamentals of Cognitive Psychology. Madison, WI: Brown & Benchmark.

Epstein, M.L., Phillips, W.D., & Johnson, S.J. (1975). Recall of related and unrelated word pairs as a function of processing level. Journal of Experimental Psychology: Human Learning and Memory, 1 (2), 149-152.

Erdelyi, M., Buschke, H., & Finkelstein, S. (1977). Hypermensia for Socratic stimuli: The growth of recall for an internally generated memory list abstracted from a series of riddles. Memory and Cognition, 5 (3), 283-286.

Erdelyi, M.H., Finklestein, S., Herrell, N., Miller, B., & Thomas, J. (1976). Coding modality vs. input modality in hypermensia: Is a rose a rose a rose? Cognition, 4 (4), 311-319.

Flannagan, D.A., & Blick, K.A. (1989). Levels of processing and the retention of word meanings. Perceptual and Motor Skills, 68 (3, Pt.2), 1123-1128.

Fletcher, C.R., & Bloom, C.P. (1988). Causal reasoning in the comprehension of simple narrative texts. Journal of Memory and Language, 27 (3), 235-244.

Gambrell, L.B., & Jawitz, P.B. (1993). Mental imagery, text illustrations, and children's story comprehension and recall. Reading Research Quarterly, 28 (3), 264-276.

Gardiner, J.M., & Java, R.I. (1993). Recognising and remembering. In Collins, A.F., Gathercole, S.E., Conway, M.A., Morris, P.E., (Eds.) Theories of memory. Hove, United Kingdom: Lawrence Erlbaum Associates.

Graf, P., & Schacter, D. (1985). Implicit and explicit memory for new associations in normal and amnesic subjects. Journal of Experimental Psychology: Learning, Memory, and Cognition, 11 (3), 501-518.

Greene, R.L. (1992). Human memory: Paradigms and paradoxes. Hillsdale, NJ: Lawrence Erlbaum Associates.

Greenwald, A.G., & Banaji, M.R. (1989). The self as a memory system: Powerful, but ordinary. Journal of Personality and Social Psychology, 57 (1), 41-54.

Hunt, R.R., & Einstein, G.O. (1981). Relational item-specific information in memory. Journal of Verbal Learning and Verbal Behavior, 20 (5), 497-514.

Hunt, R.R., & McDaniel, M.A. (1993). The enigma of organization and distinctiveness. Journal of Memory and Language, 32, (4), 421-445.

Hunt, R.R., & Seta, C.E. (1993). Category size effects in recall: The roles of individual item and relational information. Journal of Experimental Psychology: Learning, Memory, and Cognition, 10 (3), 454-464.

Karni, A., Tanne, D., Rubenstein, B.S., Askenasy, J.J.M., et al. (1994). Dependence on REM sleep of overnight improvement of a perceptual skill. Science, 265 (5172), 679-682.

Kardash, C.A., Royer, J.M., & Greene, B.A. (1988). Effects of schemata on both encoding and retrieval of information from prose. Journal of Educational Psychology, 80 (3), 324-329.

Kendzierski, D. (1980). Self-schemata and scripts: The recall of self-referent and scriptal information. Personality and Social Psychology Bulletin, 6 (1), 23-29.

Klein, S.B., Loftus, J., Kihlsteom, J.F., & Aseron, R. (1989). Effects of item specific and relational information on hypermensic recall. Journal of Experimental Psychology: Learning, Memory, and Cognition, 15 (6), 1192-1197.

Kosslyn, S.M. (1980). Image and mind. Cambridge, MA: Harvard University Press.

Mantyla, T. (1986). Optimizing cue effectiveness: Recall of 500 and 600 incidentally learned words. Journal of Experimental Psychology: Learning, Memory, and Cognition, 12 (1), 303-312.

Mantyla, T., & Nilsson, L.G. (1988). Cue distinctiveness and forgetting: Effectiveness of self-generated cues in delayed recall. Journal of Experimental Psychology: Learning, Memory, and Cognition, 14 (3), 502-529.

Menke, D.J., & Pressley, M. (1994). Elaborative interrogation: Using "why" questions to enhance the learning from text. Journal of Reading, 37 (8), 642-645.

Murphy, M.D., & Wallace, W.P. (1974). Encoding specificity: Semantic change between storage and retrieval cues. Journal of Experimental Psychology, 103 (4), 768-774.

Parkin, A.J. (1993). Memory: Phenomena, experiment, and theory. Oxford: Blackwell Publishers.

Pellegrino, J.W., & Battig, W.F. (1972). Effects of semantic list structure differences in free recall. Psychonomic Science, 29 (2), 65-67.

Penney, C.G. (1988). A beneficial effect of part-list cueing with unrelated words. Bulletin of the Psychonomic Society, 26 (4), 297-300.

Reddy, B.G., & Bellezza, F.S. (1983). Encoding specificity in free recall. Journal of Experimental Psychology: Learning, Memory, and Cognition, 9 (1),167-174.

Robins, S., & Mayer, R.E. (1993). Schema training in analogical reasoning. Journal of Educational Psychology, 85 (3), 529-538.

Roediger, H.L., & Thorpe, L.A. (1978). The role of recall time in producing hypermensia. Memory and Cognition, 6 (3), 296-305.

Roediger, H.L. III (1990). Implicit memory: A commentary. Bulletin of the Psychonomic Society, 28 (4), 373-380.

Roediger, H.L. III, & Blaxton, T.A. (1987). Retrieval modes produce dissociations in memory for surface information. In D. Gorfein, & P.R. Hoffman (Eds.) Memory and cognitive processes: The Ebbinghaus centennial conference (pp. 349-379). Hillsdale, NJ: Lawrence Erlbaum Associates Inc.

Roediger, H.L. III, Weldon, M.S., & Challis, B.H. (1989). Explaining dissociations between implicit and explicit measures of retention: A processing account. In H.L. Roediger III, & F.I.M. Craik (Eds.) Varieties of memory and consciousness: Essays in honor of Endel Tulvig. Hillsdale, NJ: Lawrence Erlbaum Associates Inc.

Rose, R.J. (1992). Degree of learning, interpolated tests, and rate of forgetting. Memory and Cognition, 20 (6), 621-632.

Rybash, J.M., & Osborne, J.L. (1991). Implicit memory, the serial position effect, and test awareness. Bulletin of the Psychonomic Society, 29 (4), 327-330.

Salz, E., & Dixon, D. (1982). Let's pretend: The role of motoric imagery in memory for sentences and words. Journal of Experimental Child Psychology, 43 (1), 77-92.

Schneider, W. (1993). Domain-specific knowledge and memory performance in children. Educational Psychology Review, 5 (3), 257-273.

Seifert, T.L. (1993). Effects of elaborative interrogation with prose passages. Journal of Educational Psychology, 85 (4), 642-651.

Semb, G.B., Ellis, J.A., & Araujo, J. (1993). Long-term memory for knowledge learned in school. Journal of Educational Psychology, 85 (2), 305-316.

Smith, C., & Lapp, L. (1991). Increases in number of REMs and REM density in humans following an itensive learning period. Sleep, 14, (4), 325-330.

Smith, C., & MacNeill, C. (1993). A paradoxical sleep-dependent window for memory 53-56 h. after the end of avoidance training. Psychobiology, 21 (2), 109-112.

Smith, S.M. (1982). Enhancement of recall using multiple environmental contexts during learning. Memory and Cognition, 10 (5), 405-412.

Tilley, A.J. (1981). Retention over a period of REM or non-REM sleep. British Journal of Psychology, 72 (2), 241-248.

Treisman, A.M., & Gelade, G. (1980). A feature intregration theory of attention. Cognitive Psychology, 12 (1), 97-136.

Tulving, E. (19985). How many memory systems are there? American Psychologist, 40 (4), 385-398.

Weldon, M.S., & Roediger, H.L. (1987). Altering retrieval demands reverses the picture superiority effect. Memory and Cognition, 15 (4), 269-280.

Wood, E., Willoughby, T., Kaspar, V., & Idle, T. (1994). Enhancing adolescents' recall of factual content: The impact of provided versus self-generated elaborations. The Alberta Journal of Educatinal Research, 40 (1), 57-65.

Wright, A.A., Cook, R.G., Rivera, J.J., Shyan, M.R., Neiworth, J.J., &Jitsumori, M. (1990). Naming, rehearsal, and interstumulus interval effects in memory processing. Journal of Experimental Psychology: Learning, Memory and Cognition, 16 (6), 1043-1059.

Yekovich, F.R., & Thorndyke, P.W. (1981). An evaluation of alternative functional models of narrative schemata. Journal of Verbal Learning and Verbal Behavior, 20 (4), 454-469.